The Oxford English Programme 2

John Seely
Frank Green
David Kitchen

Steve Barlow
Richard Bates
Graham Nutbrown
Steve Skidmore
Christopher Stubbs

Oxford University Press

Contents

PART A Stories, poems, and specials

Some people

By sea and land

PART B Using words

Speaking and listening

Reading

Writing

Presentation

Part A

Stories, poems, and specials

The great leap-frog contest

Rosie Mahoney was a tough little Irish kid. She had little use for girls, and as far as possible avoided them. She had less use for boys, but found it undesirable to avoid them. That is to say, she made it a point to take part in everything the boys did. She was always on hand, and always the first to take up any daring or crazy idea. She liked being in on any mischief the boys might have in mind, and she wanted to play on any teams they organised.

As a matter of fact, she was just naturally the equal of any boy in the neighbourhood, and much the superior of many of them. Especially after she had lived in the neighbourhood three years. It took her that long to make everybody understand that she had come to stay and that she was going to stay.

She did, too; even after the arrival of a boy named Rex Folger, who was from somewhere in the south of Texas. This boy Rex was a natural-born leader. Two months after his arrrival in the neighbourhood, it was understood by everyone that if Rex wasn't the leader of the gang, he was very nearly the leader. He had fought and licked every boy in the neighbourhood who at one time or another had fancied himself leader. And he had done so without any noticeable ill-feeling, pride, or ambition.

As a matter of fact, no one could possibly have been more good-natured than Rex. Everybody resented him, just the same.

One winter, the whole neighbourhood took to playing a game that had become popular on the other side of the track, in another slum neighbourhood of the town: Leapfrog. The idea was for as many boys as cared to participate to bend down and be leaped over by every other boy in the game, and then himself to get up and begin leaping over all the other boys, and then bend down again until all the boys had leaped over him again, and keep this up until all the other players had become exhausted. This didn't happen, sometimes, until the last two players had travelled a distance of three or four miles, while the other players walked along, watching and making bets.

Rosie, of course, was always in on the game. She was always one of the last to drop out, too. And she was the only person in the neighbourhood Rex Folger hadn't fought and beaten.

He felt that that was much too humiliating even to think about. But inasmuch as she seemed to be a member of the gang, he felt that in some way or another he ought to prove his superiority.

One summer day during vacation, an argument between Rex and Rosie developed and Rosie pulled off her turtle-neck sweater and challenged him to a fight. Rex took a cigarette from his pocket, lighted it, inhaled, and told Rosie he wasn't in the habit of hitting women – where he came from that amounted to boxing your mother. On the other hand, he said, if Rosie cared to compete with him in any other sport, he would be very glad to oblige her. Rex was a very calm and courteous conversationalist. He had a poise. It was unconscious, of course, but he had it just the same. He was just naturally a man who couldn't be hurried, flustered, or excited.

So Rex and Rosie fought it out in this game Leapfrog. They got to leaping over one another, quickly, too, until the first thing we knew the whole gang of us was out on the State Highway going south towards Fowler. It was a very hot day. Rosie and Rex were in great shape, and it looked like one was tougher than the other and more stubborn. They talked a good deal, especially Rosie, who insisted that she would have to fall down unconscious before she'd give up to a guy like Rex.

He said he was sorry his opponent was a girl. It grieved him deeply to have to make a girl exert herself to the point of death, but it was just too bad. He had to, so he had to. They leaped and squatted, leaped and squatted, and we got to Sam Day's vineyard. That was half-way to Fowler. It didn't seem like either Rosie or Rex was ever going to get tired. They hadn't even begun to show signs of growing tired, although each of them was sweating a great deal.

Naturally, we were sure Rex would win the contest. But that was because we hadn't taken into account the fact that he was a simple person, whereas Rosie was crafty and shrewd. Rosie knew how to figure angles. She had discovered how to jump over Rex Folger in a way that weakened him. And after a while, about three miles out of Fowler, we noticed that she was coming down on Rex's neck, instead of on his back. Naturally, this was hurting him and making the blood rush to his head. Rosie herself squatted in such a way that it was impossible, almost, for Rex to get anywhere near her neck with his hands.

Before long, we noticed that Rex was weakening. His head was getting closer and closer to the ground. About a half mile out of Fowler, we heard Rex's head bumping the ground every time Rosie leaped over him.

They were good loud bumps that we knew were painful, but Rex wasn't complaining. He was too proud to complain.

Rosie, on the other hand, knew she had her man, and was giving him all she had. She was bumping his head on the ground as solidly as she could, because she knew she didn't have much more fight in her, and if she didn't lay him out cold, in the hot sun, in the next ten minutes or so, she would fall down exhausted herself, and lose the contest.

It looked pretty bad for the boy from Texas. We couldn't understand how he could take so much punishment. We all felt that Rex was getting what he had coming to him, but at the same time everybody seemed to feel badly about Rosie, a girl, doing the job instead of one of us. Of course, that was where we were wrong. Nobody but Rosie could have figured out that smart way of humiliating a very powerful and superior boy. It was probably the woman in her.

Less than a hundred yards from the heart of Fowler, Rosie, with great and admirable artistry, finished the job. That was where the dirt of the highway siding ended and the paved main street of Fowler began. This street was paved with cement, not asphalt. Asphalt, in that heat, would have been too soft to serve, but cement had exactly the right degree of brittleness. I think Rex, when he squatted over the hard cement, knew the game was up. But he was brave to the end. He squatted over the hard cement and waited for the worst. Behind him, Rosie Mahoney prepared to make the supreme effort. In this next leap, she intended to give her all, which she did.

8

She came down on Rex Folger's neck like a ton of bricks. His head banged against the hard cement, his body straightened out, and his arms and legs twitched.

He was out like a light.

Six paces in front of him, Rosie Mahoney squatted and waited. Jim Telesco counted twenty, which was the time allowed for each leap. Rex didn't get up during the count.

The contest was over. The winner of the contest was Rosie Mahoney.

Rex didn't get up by himself at all. He just stayed where he was until a half-dozen of us lifted him and carried him to a horse trough, where we splashed water on his face.

Rex was a confused young man all the way home. He was also a deeply humiliated one. He couldn't understand anything about anything. He just looked dazed and speechless. Every now and then we imagined he wanted to talk, and I guess he did, but after we'd all gotten ready to hear what he had to say, he couldn't speak. He made a gesture so tragic that tears came to the eyes of eleven members of the gang.

Rosie Mahoney, on the other hand, talked all the way home. She said everything.

I think it made a better man of Rex. More human. After that he was a gentler sort of soul. It may have been because he couldn't see very well for some time. At any rate, for weeks, he seemed to be going around in a dream. He took little part in the activities of the gang, and the following winter he stayed away altogether.

That winter Rosie Mahoney stopped hanging around with the gang, too. She had a flair for making an exit at the right time.

William Saroyan

Fruit

Some things are true
And some are only true in school.
Like fruit. We did fruit
Today in Science. We learnt
A tomato's a fruit but
A strawberry isn't.
I copied down the diagrams
And all the notes
'Cos I knew I had to
Pretend it was true.
I'm not daft, I know when
to make-believe:
That's why I'm
Set One for Science.

Mick Gowar

a tomato is a fruit

...but a strawberry isn't

Nobody wants a poet in their team

Reds
We'll have Watson
Dusty Walters
Barney's brother
We'll have Perkins

We'll have Spaggot
We'll have 'turnip'
We've got Curtis
We've got Wayne

We'll have Sturgiss
We've got Robbins
We've got worst side
You have East

East is useless
We'll swap East for Nigel Worth
Come here Worthy, on our side
No! change with Nipper, he's just arrived.

You play this way
Three goals change,
and who
is that...?

Blues
....We'll have Piles
Norman Eyles
Porky Day
We've got Ray

....We'll have Spud
We'll have Cud
We've got Mick
And you've got Dick

....You have Tone
We've got Bones
You've got best!
And we'll have West

....Bugs is worse

....We'll play that

You can have him

Peter Dixon

Buy fiddly hi-fi, dumb chum

Characters

Anthony (13 year old boy)	Louise (13 year old girl)
Marlon (13 year old boy)	Manager/ess
Fatty (13 year old girl)	Sales-person

(*Scene: a High Street electronics store* – **Anthony** *enters followed by* **Marlon, Fatty** *and* **Louise**. *The* **Manager/ess** *and a* **Sales-person** *are fussing with the display or attending to another* **Customer**.)

Ant: ...And I'll tell you another thing, brick bonce, I'm never going to lend you anything again.

Marlon: But it wasn't my fault. I keep telling you, but you just won't listen.

Ant: Whose fault was it then, Genius? I let you borrow my walkman for half an hour and you bring it back bust.

Fatty: How did you do that, then?

Marlon: I don't know. Maybe Pete got hold of it.

Fatty: You mean your brother?

Marlon: Yeah.

Louise: That's a good one, blaming your younger brother.

Fatty: My older sister always blames me for everything. I get into awful trouble sometimes.

Louise: Don't you tell your mum and dad that it's her?

Fatty: Yes, but they don't always believe me.

Louise: I usually put the blame on our dogs – they can't answer back!

Ant: Maybe you could put the blame on your hamster, Marlon – perhaps he got bored spinning on his wheel and wanted to listen to some heavy metal music, so he puts on the headphones, starts head-banging and smashes my walkman against his water bowl.
(**Fatty** *and* **Louise** *laugh at this.*)

Marlon: Ha ha, very funny – look, I'm telling you for the last time, I didn't bust it.

Ant: And I'm telling you for the last time that my walkman hasn't worked ever since you gave it back to me.

Marlon: Well, Pete probably poured orange juice in it...

Ant: Orange juice??

Marlon: That's what he usually does. He's stupid.

Louise: Sounds as if he takes after you.

Fatty: *(Interested)* Didn't you say he poured milk into your video?

Marlon: Sometimes it's milk...

Ant: I don't care what it was, the point is it's wrecked my stereo.

Marlon: Alright, I've said I'll pay for it to be mended.

Ant: No, I've said you'll pay for it to be mended.

Louise: Cor, they've got some smart gear in here. Look at those computers and the video stuff.

Fatty: Hey, Louise, smile, you're on camera.

Louise: Where? Oh, yeah. Look, Ant, we're all on Telly.

(All crowd round the TV screen.)

Fatty: Where's the video camera?

Louise: There it is, up there.

(The four of them face the camera and start pulling faces at it.)

Fatty: Don't look at the camera, Marl, you'll probably break the lens.

Marlon: Get lost.

Fatty: It's just like being on television.

Marlon: We are on television.

Fatty: You know what I mean.

*(**Ant** stands in front of the camera in the pose of a news reporter.)*

Ant: Here we are at Clickons, the electrical shop where I am reporting on an attempted murder.

Marlon: Attempted murder? Whose?

Ant: *(Own voice)* Yours! If I don't get this fixed! *(Reporter's voice)* The shop is very quiet at the moment, but a sense of danger hangs in the air...at any moment, violence could break out...

Fatty: Look out, somebody's coming over.

Ant: *(Very quickly)* This is Anthony Sissons, for News At Ten, about to kill Marlon if my walkman isn't mended.
(The Sales-person approaches them.)

SP: Can I help you?

Marlon: Yeah, stop him killing me.

SP: What?

Fatty: He's only joking.

Ant: No, I'm not.

Louise: *(Offering the stereo)* Can you repair this please?

SP: Oh, dear oh dear. *(Takes the stereo between thumb and forefinger and holds it at arm's length as if it were something he has found in the gutter.)* What is it?

Ant: *(Proudly)* It's a Mankibuji VT 962 PS.

SP: It's a bit sticky, isn't it?

Louise: Yeah, well – can you fix it?

SP: What's wrong with it?
(**Louise, Marlon, Ant** and **Fatty** *look at her/him and each other as if the* **Sales-person** *has gone mad.*)

Fatty: *(Very patiently, as if to a small child.)* It's not working.

SP: Yes, I gathered that – I meant – oh, never mind. Lesley, can you spare a moment? *(The* **Manager/ess** *comes over.)* Can we repair this?

Manager/ess: *(Looking it over)* Oh dear. Tut tut. Not a hope, I'm afraid.

Ant: Marlon, prepare to die.
(**Marlon, Ant, Fatty** and **Louise** *look worried.*)

Fatty: Why can't you fix it?

Manager/ess: Well, it's last year's model.

Marlon: That's because he bought it last year.

Manager/ess: Quite – of course, you knew that it had been replaced by the TTFN 6345X, didn't you?

Ant: *(Who didn't)* Oh, yeah – sure.

Manager/ess: Well, there you are.

Louise: Where are we?

SP: We can't get the parts anymore.

Manager/ess: Anyway, what's wrong with it?

Marlon, Louise and **Fatty:** *(Together)* It's not working!!

Ant: *(Hurriedly)* They mean, the tape doesn't go round...

Manager/ess: Sounds like the commutator...

Marlon: And there's no sound coming out...

SP: Could be the diodes...

Louise: And none of the buttons work...

Manager/ess: Probably the transistors.

Ant: *(Trying to impress)* Couldn't be the valves, could it?

Manager/ess: *(Pityingly)* They don't use valves in personal stereos, sir.

(**Ant** *is crushed.*)

Fatty: Well, at least we know what it isn't.

(**Ant** *kicks her.*)

Louise: You mean you can't get any parts for it?

Manager/ess: Well, we'd have to send to Taiwan. In any case, this uses a microchip. They're no longer available; the new models use a minimicrochip.

Marlon: Vinegar!

Louise: What?

Marlon: I'll bet that's what my brother poured into it – vinegar to go on all those chips.

Louise: Shut up, Marlon, that joke was pathetic.

SP: Even if it could be repaired, it would probably be cheaper to buy a new one.

Ant: Oh, great!

Marlon: Hey, I'm not buying you a new one!

SP: You see, this model went out with the dinosaurs.

Ant: I only bought it last year.

Manager/ess: Quite. But this sort of technology continues to develop at a rapid pace. A week is a long time in stereo systems, sir, and your personal stereo isn't really State of the Art.

Louise: (*Quietly to* **Fatty** *and* **Marlon**) It's not in much of a state at all with orange juice in it.

Ant: How do you mean, not State of the Art?

SP: Well, sir, if you want to buy a personal stereo these days, it MUST have auto-reverse, Dolby NR, AM, FM, varispeed, dual headphones, and Solar panels. Why, your model hasn't even got QLDSDPS.

Ant: Hasn't it?

Marlon: What's QLD whatsits?

Manager/ess: Quartz Locked Digitally Synthesized Drive Preset.

(*The kids still look confused.*)

Fatty: What's that then?

Ant: (*Still trying to impress*) Well, it's obvious, isn't it?

Louise: Go on then, clever clogs, what does it do?

Ant: (*No idea*) Well, it locks the quarter...er...and sympathises with your digits.

Marlon: Oh yeah? What about the drive preset?

Ant: Ah...well...that's so when you take it in the car, you can set it to play before you start to drive. (*To* **Sales-person** *and* **Manager/ess**) Right?

Manager/ess: (*Raising eyes to heaven*) Close sir, very close.

SP: Of course, you know what you get if you don't have a quartz locked digitally synthesized drive preset, don't you?

Ant: (*Nervous*) Er – what?

SP: (*After looking round confidentially*) Wow!

(**Marlon, Fatty** *and* **Louise** *look at each other, say,* 'Wow!' *and giggle.*)

Ant: Eh?

SP And...flutter!
  (**Marlon, Louise** and **Fatty** *imitate birds, fluttering their hands and whistling until a look from the* **Manager/ess** *stops them.*)
Ant: Getaway! Er – is that bad?
  (**Sales-person** and **Manager/ess** *laugh heartily –* **Ant** *joins in – he's no idea why.*)
Manager/ess: Oh, very funny, sir.
Ant: Er, yeah, right.
SP: Now, take a look at this, sir. (*Takes another stereo off the display.*) This is a Hamsarni 940 SWALK.
Ant: Good is it?
SP: Well, as long as you're replacing your stereo, sir, you'll want to go up-market, won't you?
Ant: I don't want one from the market, they fall to bits, I want one from here.
Manager/ess: That is to say, you'll want a better one.
Ant: Oh, 'course.
Marlon: I've told you, I'm not buying you a new one.
SP: Now, the Hamsarni has a graphic equaliser.
Ant: (*Still trying to be clever*) Yes, well, you've got to have your graphics equalised, haven't you?
SP: Er, quite...and Auto-reverse, and Dolby, fine stereo imaging, and a very clear top end...

16

Louise: (*Peering into* **Marlon's** *ear*) Marlon's got a clear top end
   – there's nothing in there.

SP: ...and a clearly revealed bottom end...

Louise: It sounds like when your trousers split, Ant.

Ant: Shut up! I'm trying to concentrate.

Fatty: (*Sympathetically*) Does it hurt?

SP: (*Desperately*) In fact, you get very clear sound. And why?

Ant: Er – why?

SP: Because of the on-board speakers. You see, most personal stereos
   only have a single speaker unit, but this one has two. Not only does it
   have a woofer...
   (**Louise**, **Marlon** *and* **Fatty** *imitate dogs, giggling.*)

SP: It also has a tweeter.
   (**Louise**, **Marlon** *and* **Fatty** *go back to the bird imitations.*)

Ant: Shut up! Er, yeah, very impressive. How much?

Manager/ess: Two hundred and forty pounds, fifty pence, sir.
   (**Ant**, **Marlon**, **Louise** *and* **Fatty** *gasp in astonishment.*)

Marlon: If you think I'm paying out that much, you can get lost!

Manager/ess: Would you like to try it, sir?

Ant: Ah, yeah, sure.
   (*He tries it on.* **Manager/ess** *offers tape.* **Ant** *puts it in and switches
   music on. The volume is too loud!* **Ant** *is in agony – he turns the
   volume down. Listens, starts to nod and jig to music.*)

Louise: Let's have a listen. (*Snatches it off* **Ant** *– starts to jig*) Hey,
   sound.

Marlon: Give us a listen. *(Takes it: jigs)* Good, innit?

Fatty: What about me? *(Takes it: jigs)* Hey, it's nice.

Ant: *(Snatching it back)* When you've quite finished.
(*To* **Sales-person**) Yeah, nice, it's just that it's a bit expensive.

SP: Only in one sense, sir – the initial outlay may be a bit steep, but you'll find the running costs much lower...

Marlon: Running costs?

SP: You see, this model takes batteries which are recharged by the rays of the sun.

Louise: What happens if it rains?

Manager/ess: *(Ignoring* **Louise***)* A solar cell creates the power to recharge the batteries, so you need never buy another set! Let me see what sort of batteries your stereo runs off, and I'll work out the saving you'll make.
(**Manager/ess** *opens* **Ant's** *machine. It has no batteries inside. There is a silence.*)

Manager/ess: There don't appear to be any batteries in here.

Fatty: So that's why it's not working!

Louise: *(To* **Ant***)* You great wally! Why didn't you look?

Ant: *(Hurt)* Why yell at me? It's his brother's fault.

Marlon: He must've nicked the batteries to put in his Lego.

Ant: Well, you can get me some more batteries then.

Manager/ess: Does that mean you don't want to buy the Hamsarni?

Ant: There's no point, is there?

SP: But what about the wow?

Manager/ess: And flutter?

SP: And the QLDSDPS?

Louise: He'll manage without it. He only wants to listen to tapes, not pick up Satellite TV.

Marlon: Exactly. Just four batteries, please.

SP: *(Annoyed but trying not to show it.)* Certainly. What type would you like? Cadmium? Long Life Silver? Long Life Gold? Zinc Oxide? Long Life Zinc Oxide? Long Life Zinc Oxide with Cadmium...?

Fatty: *(Grabbing two battery packs off the display.)* Just two of these, please.

SP: That'll be two pounds fifty.
(**Ant** *looks at* **Marlon***, who pays up.* **Ant** *puts the batteries into his old cassette and switches it on.*)

Ant: Hey, it works!
(*He starts to sing along to one of the current hits – the others join in and jig about.*)

SP: *(Through gritted teeth)* Thank you.

Manager/ess: *(Sarcastically)* Have a nice day.

Steve Barlow and *Steve Skidmore*

The great leap-frog contest

First impressions

1 When you read the story, what were the main things that struck you about Rosie Mahoney?
2 What were your first impressions of Rex Folger?

Second thoughts

Now read the story again and think about these points. Make sure that you can find the part(s) of the story that tell(s) you about each one.

1 What happened when Rex moved to the neighbourhood.
2 What Rex thought about girls.
3 The way in which Rosie is described at the beginning of the story.
4 What Rosie thought about girls – and boys.
5 Why Rex felt he had to beat Rosie.
6 Why Rosie had to beat Rex.
7 The way in which Rosie set out to win – and what you think of it.
8 What this tells us about Rosie's character.
9 The way in which Rex didn't seem to be able to do anything about it.
10 What this tells us about his character.

Boys and girls

This story was written some years ago and is not set in Britain. Think about how it describes the attitudes of people towards boys and girls and how they should behave. Do people you know have similar attitudes? If not, how do they differ?

Fruit

Writing

'Some things...are only true in school' – can you think of any other examples? Make a list of things that are 'only true in school'.

Choose one or more of your ideas as the basis for a piece of writing:
● a short poem like *Fruit*
● a story called 'Only true at school'

Nobody wants a poet in their team

Group work – reading aloud

This poem is made for reading aloud...but first of all you've got to work out how to read it.

1 Read it through on your own.
2 Talk about it in your group:
   ● How many voices does it need?
   ● How should the lines be divided between the voices?
   ● Who would be getting noisier or more excited and when?
   ● How should the lines be spoken?
3 Divide the poem up between the readers in the group.
4 Practise reading it aloud.
5 Act it out.

Buy fiddly hi-fi, dumb chum

Thinking about the play

Marlon borrows Ant's stereo and when he returns it, it is not working. Have you ever borrowed something and broken it? Suppose that this did happen, what would you do:

1 Hide it?
2 Pretend that it wasn't you who broke it?
3 Deny all knowledge of it?
4 Own up?

Ant is nearly persuaded to buy the personal stereo recommended by the sales-person.

5 How does the sales-person go about trying to sell Ant the stereo?
6 Have you ever been pressured into buying something you didn't really want or need?

The sales-person and manager use a lot of technical terms when they describe the personal stereos. This is sometimes called jargon.

7 Can you think of other jobs or areas of life where people use jargon?
8 How many other examples of jargon can you think of?

Role play

Pairs: Complaints

Label yourselves **A** and **B**. The role play is set in a shop. Decide what kind of shop.

Role A: You are a customer bringing back something you bought at the shop. You think it is faulty. You either want a new one, or your money back. Decide what it is and what is wrong with it.

Role B: You are the shop assistant. You do not want to supply a new item or to give the customer's money back.

Starter: A says, 'I bought this from this shop yesterday.'

Groups: Supersell!

1 Find a useless object : a broken biro, one left shoe, a used piece of rough paper – use your imagination!
2 Choose one member of the group to be the sales-person.
3 The sales-person has to try to sell the 'product' to the rest of the group.
4 When the sales-person has succeeded (or failed) repeat with a new object and a new sales-person.

Groups: Verbal boxing

1 Choose two 'boxers': **A** and **B**
2 Give them a topic. Start with this one: **A** has borrowed a cassette from **B** and returned it damaged. **A** wants a new one. **B** is refusing. Both have good reasons.
3 **A** and **B** have one minute to argue about this.
4 When the minute is up, the rest of the group vote for the person who has given the best argument.
5 The winner becomes champion and takes on a new challenger. The rest of the group think of a new topic.

Rules
● No bad language.
● No threats.
● No touching the other person.
● If either of the two breaks the rules, that person is disqualified.

Best buy!

Discussion points

1. What are the pleasures of owning a personal stereo?
2. What sort of people love personal stereos?
3. What are the disadvantages of using personal stereos?
4. Are there any people who hate personal stereos?

Writing

1. Draw up a table, of the reasons people give for being in favour of personal stereos, and against them.
2. Use it to help you decide which side has the best argument.
3. Write a short explanation of what you have decided and why.

Buy me! ♪♫

NEW!

SUPERB PERFORMANCE
with this smart 3 band graphic equaliser radio cassette player. *You must hear it to believe it.*

Technology at its best
A.M./F.M.; fast forward and rewind, auto-stop and auto-reverse for continuous playback.
So easy to use.

Great value
at this introductory offer of

£29.95 including headphones.

AN EXCELLENT CHOICE!

If you wanted to buy a personal stereo there are hundreds to choose from. Advertisements like these might help you to make up your mind.

Sometimes we have to separate fact (3 band graphic equaliser) from opinion (superb performance). Copy and complete the table below.

Questions

1 Which advertisement is most likely to attract a customer? Why?
2 Which advertisement is most useful to a customer? Why?

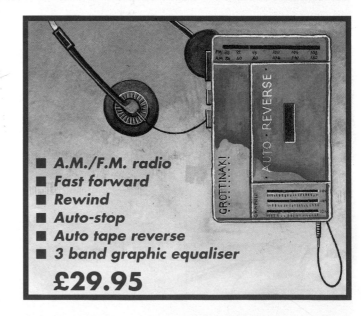

- ■ **A.M./F.M. radio**
- ■ **Fast forward**
- ■ **Rewind**
- ■ **Auto-stop**
- ■ **Auto tape reverse**
- ■ **3 band graphic equaliser**

£29.95

	Mankibuji VT 966 PS	Grottinaki 216S
Facts		
Opinions		
Price		

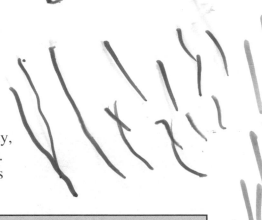

Buy which?

People say that you get what you pay for; meaning that the more you pay, the better the article. Consumer reports show that this is not always true. Here is a consumer report on personal radio cassettes. The results of this are summarised on page 24.

Personal stereos: *the facts and figures*

1 Price

These are the lowest widely available prices we found. Manufacturer's recommended prices are given in italics.

2 Features

An autostop (A) stops the mechanism at the end of a tape, which saves batteries and wear. Most of the players in our test have a rewind facility (B). Not having rewind can be inconvenient. On-ear mini headphones (D) rest on the ears. In-ear headphones (E) don't usually have a headband: they fit directly into the ears. In-ear sideways headphones (F) have a headband, but our users found them much more uncomfortable than other types.

Reverse play lets you switch to the other side of the tape without having to remove the cassette from the player. With manual reverse (G) you can do this any time, auto-reverse (H) does it automatically at the end of the tape. The tape type switch (I) on a personal stereo is effectively a tone control which will give you more or less treble; the graphic equaliser (K) does the same job, but with a greater range of adjustment. Dolby B noise reduction (P) cuts down on tape hiss. The FM aerials on personal stereo radios are formed by the wire to the headphones, and this often means that there's hiss and fading when listening to FM in stereo, especially

on the move. Switching to mono gives better results. A stereo indicator light (S) shows that you're receiving a stereo broadcast.

3 Weight

Weights are for player with batteries, clip and case, where provided. We haven't included headphones; typically these weigh around 50g.

4 Size

Average size of players in this test was 125 x 90 x 40 mm.

5 Optional accessories

These are the manufacturers' optional extras you can buy to add to the players we tested. The car battery cord (b) lets you power the player from the cigarette lighter of a car – but it's not advisable for drivers to use personal stereos. Active speakers (d) have built-in amplifiers. This means the player can be used like a stereo radio recorder. A two-way headphone (f) lets two people listen to the player at once.

6 Sound quality

A panel of listeners rated each player using pre-recorded tapes and the headphones supplied with it. We then combined these ratings with the results of a range of technical tests to produce an overall score. We did similar sound quality tests on both AM and FM for music and speech.

7 Running costs

We measured the amount of current each player used when playing a tape at a comfortable volume, and calculated running costs. These varied from under 4p an hour to over 8p.

8 Ease of use

We examined each personal stereo to see how easy it was to insert a tape and to replace batteries. We looked at the labelling and operation of the controls, and how comfortable it was to wear.

We also looked at how easy it was to tune the radio. Many of the models had tuning controls that were difficult to use and read.

9 Sound leakage

This is the tinny sound heard by people other than the user. We assessed each headphone set to see how 'personal' the personal stereo was.

10 Jogging

We conducted a jogging test to see how the movement caused by running affected tape speed and sound quality.

Other tests

Radio reception
Rewind times
Reduced voltage
Reliability

🎵 The facts

	Price £ 1	Features (see Key) 2	Weight (see Key) 3	Size (see Key) 4	Optional Accessories (see Key) 5	6 Sound quality Tape	FM	AM	Running costs (see Key) 7	Ease of use 8	Sound leakage 9	Jogging 10
1	70	BDHIKLP	III	II	adef	◕	◑	◑	£	◕	◑	
2	25	ADKLS	II	III		◑	◑	◑	££	◔	◔	
3	25	ADKLS	II	III	f	◑	◑	◑	££	◔	◔	◗
4	90	ABEHIKLPS	III	II	a	◑	◕	◑	££	◑	◑	◕
5	28	ADKLS	II	III		◑	◑	◑	££	◔	◔	◕
6	40	ABLS	III	III	ab	◔	◑	◔	££	◑	◑	
7	25	ADKLS	II	III		◑	◑	◑	££	◔	◔	◕
8	30	ABDKLS	III	III		◑	◑	◑	££	◑	○	
9	40	ABDHKL	II	II		◔	◑	◔	££	◑	◔	◗
10	90	ABFIKLP	I	III	abcd	◑	◑	◔	££	◔	◕	
11	35	ABDKLS	II	III	a	*	◕	◑	££	◑	◑	◕
12	60	ABDGHIKLP	III	III	a	◕	◕	◑	£	◑	◑	

Key

Features

A = autostop
B = rewind
C = rechargeable battery
D = on-ear mini headphones
E = in-ear headphones
F = in-ear sideways headphones
G = manual reverse
H = auto-reverse
I = tape type switch
J = built-in rechargeable battery
K = graphic equaliser
L = belt clip
P = Dolby B
Q = case with belt loop
S = stereo indicator light

Weight (gm)

I = up to 270
II = up to 310
III = up to 350

Size (cm)

I = up to 11 x 9 x 3
II = up to 12 x 9 x 4
III = up to 14 x 9 x 5

Running costs

£ = up to 6p per hour
££ = up to 9p per hour

Optional accessories

a = mains adaptor
b = car battery cord
c = battery case
d = active speakers
e = rechargeable batteries
f = two-way headphone adaptor
* = not rated for tape listening

KEY TO RATINGS   ● ◕ ◑ ◔ ○   best ←→ worst

Questions

1 Which sets have more bad results ○ than good ● ?
2 Do any sets have an equal number of bad and good results?
3 Which sets have more good results than bad?
4 Based on these results, and also taking into account the information in columns 1, 2, 5 and 7: which personal radio cassette(s) do you think represent(s) good value for money?
5 What are the reasons for your choice?

Writing

Compose an honest advertisement, including an illustration, for one of the sets tested here.

Personal stereos *Which? August 1988*

Noulded into the shake of a goat

When I was a tall, sensitive boy at school. I once sent up for a booklet about how to be a ventriloquist.

I was always 'sending up' for things – variable focus lamps, propelling pencils with choice of six differently coloured leads, air pistols discharging wooden bullets, scale model tanks with genuine caterpillar action, tricks in glass topped boxes, and so on – anything, I suppose, to vary the monotony of straight games and education.

The booklet arrived at breakfast time one morning in a large square envelope. I told the other boys it was a new stamp album, and got on with my shredded liver poached in water. I wanted the voice throwing to come as a real surprise.

We had twenty minutes after breakfast in which to get our things ready for first school. I had a quick run through the new book.

It was called *Ventriloquism in Three Weeks*. On the first page it explained that ventriloquism came from the Latin *ventriloquus* – 'a speaking from the belly'. There was also a drawing of a schoolboy smiling pleasantly at a railway porter carrying a trunk. From the trunk came hysterical cries of 'Help! Help! Murder! Police!'

It was just the sort of thing I was aiming at. I slipped the book in with my other ones, and hurried off to the first school.

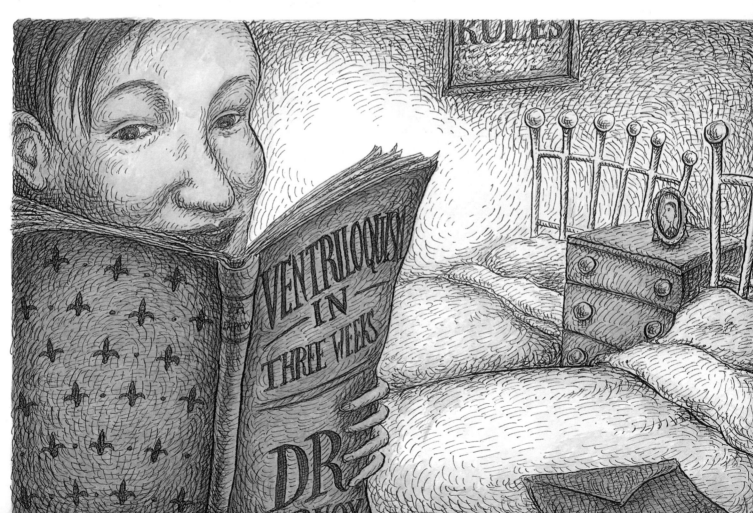

In the next fortnight I put in a good deal of practice, sitting right at the back of the class, watching my lips in a small piece of mirror, and murmuring, 'Dah, dee, day, di, doy, doo.'

It was necessary, however, to be rather careful. Dr Farvox, the author of the book, suggested that it might be as well to perform the earlier exercises 'in the privacy of one's bedroom or den'. Dr Farvox was afraid that 'chums or relatives' might laugh, particularly when one was practising the 'muffled voice in the box'.

The best way to get this going, Dr Farvox said, was to experiment 'with a continuous grunting sound in a high key, straining from the chest as if in pain.'

He was right in thinking that this exercise ought to be performed in the privacy of the bedroom. It was inclined to be noisy – so noisy, indeed, that I was twice caught straining in a high key during practical chemistry, and had to pretend that I'd been overcome by the fumes of nitric acid.

But in the end, it was the easy, pleasant smile that terminated my study of what Dr Farvox described as 'this amusing art'.

It happened one Saturday morning, in the hour before lunch, ordinarily a pleasant enough period devoted to constitutional history. Bill the Bull, who took the class, was usually fairly mellow with the prospect of the weekend before him, and there was not much need to do any work.

As was by now my invariable custom I was seated at the back of the room with a large pile of books in front of me. I was working on the Whisper Voice, which had been giving me a considerable amount of difficulty.

'Lie down, Neddy, lie down,' I whispered, watching my lips closely in the glass.

'It's due in dock at nine o'clock.'

Not bad.

'Take Ted's Kodak down to Roy.'

There it was again – the old familiar twitch on 'Kodak.'

I sat back, relaxing a little. Dr Farvox was strongly in favour of the smile. 'What the young student,' he said, 'should aim at from the first is an easy and natural expression. He should smile.'

I smiled. Smiling, I whispered, 'Take Ted's Kodak down to Roy.'

To my absolute horror I found myself smiling straight into the face of Bill the Bull.

He stopped dead. He was in the middle of something about the growth of common law, but my smile stopped him dead in his tracks.

'Well, well,' said Bill, after a moment. 'How charming. And good morning to you, too.'

I at once buried my face in my books, and tried to shove the mirror and *Ventriloquism in Three Weeks* on one side.

Bill rolled slowly down the passageway between the desks. He was an enormous Welshman with a bullet head, and very greasy, straight black hair. He took a subtle and delicate pleasure in driving the more impressionable amongst us half mad with fear at least five days a week.

'Such pretty teeth,' said Bill. 'How nice of you to smile at me. I have always wanted to win your admiration.'

The other boys sat back. They knew they were on to something good.

I kept my head lowered. I'd actually succeeded in opening my consitutional history somewhere in the middle, but the corner of Dr Farvox was clearly visible under a heap of exercise books.

Bill reached my desk. 'But who knows,' he said, 'perhaps you love me too. Perchance you've been sitting there all morning just dreaming of a little home – just you and I. And later, perhaps some little ones...'

A gasp of incredulous delight came from the other boys. This was Bill at his very best.

I looked up. It was no longer possible to pretend I thought he was talking to someone else.

'I'm sorry, sir,' I said, 'I was just smiling.'

Suddenly, Bill pounced. He snatched up Dr Farvox.

'Cripes,' he said. 'What in the world have we here? *Ventriloquism in Three Weeks*?'

'Scholars,' he said, 'be so good as to listen to this.'

He read aloud: 'To imitate a fly. Close the lips tight at one corner. Fill that cheek full of wind and force it through the aperture. Make the sound suddenly loud, and then softer, which will make it appear as though the insect were flying in different parts of the room. The illusion may be helped out by the performer chasing the imaginary fly, and flapping at it with his handkerchief.'

'Strewth,' said Bill. He looked round the class. 'We'd better get ourselves a little bit of this. Here am I taking up your time with the monotonies of constitutional history, while in this very room we have a trained performer who can imitate a fly.'

Suddenly he caught me by the back of the neck. 'Come,' he said, 'my little love, and let us hear this astounding impression.'

He dragged me down to the dais.

'Begin,' said Bill. 'Be so kind as to fill your cheek with wind and at all costs do not omit the flapping of the handkerchief.'

'Sir,' I said, 'that's animal noises. I haven't got that far yet.'

'Sir,' squeaked Bill in a high falsetto, 'that's animal noises. I 'aven't got that far yet.'

He surveyed the convulsed class calmly.

'Come, come,' he said, 'this art is not as difficult as I had imagined it to be. Did anyone see my lips move?'

They cheered him. They banged the lids of their desks. 'Try it again, sir,' they cried. 'It's splendid!'

Bill raised his hand. 'Gentlemen,' he said, 'I thank you for your kindness. I am, however, but an amateur. Am I not right in thinking we would like to hear something more from Professor Smallpox?'

They cheered again. Someone shouted, 'Make him sing a song, sir!'

Bill turned to me. 'Can you,' he said, 'Professor Smallpox, sing a song?'

It was the worst thing that had happened to me in my life. I tried to extricate myself.

'No, sir,' I said. 'I haven't mastered the labials yet.'

Bill started back. He pressed his hand to his heart.

'No labials?' he said. 'You have reached the age of fifteen without having mastered the labials. But, dear Professor Smallpox, we must look into this. Perhaps you would be so kind as to give us some outline of your difficulties?'

I picked up *Ventriloquism in Three Weeks*. There was no way out.

'There's a sentence here, sir, that goes "A pat of butter moulded into the shape of a boat".'

Bill inclined his head. 'Is there, indeed? A most illuminating remark. You propose to put it to music?'

'No, sir,' I said. 'I'm just trying to show you how hard it is. You see, you have to call that "A cat of gutter noulded into the shake of a goat".'

Bill fell right back into his chair.

'You have to call it what?' he said.

'A cat of gutter, sir, noulded into the shake of a goat.'

Bill's eyes bulged. 'Professor,' he said, 'you astound me. You bewilder me. A cat of gutter –' he repeated it reverently, savouring every syllable.

Then he sprang up. 'But we must hear this,' he cried. 'We must have this cat of gutter delivered by someone who knows what he is at. This – this is valuable stuff.'

He caught me by the ear. 'Professor,' he said, 'why does it have to be noulded into the shake of a goat?'

'Well, sir' I said, 'if you say it like that you don't have to move your lips. You sort of avoid the labials.'

'To be sure you do,' said Bill. 'Why didn't I think of it myself? Well, now, we will have a demonstration.'

He turned to face the class. 'Gentlemen,' he said, 'Professor Smallpox will now say "a pat of butter moulded into the shape of a boat" without moving his lips. I entreat your closest attention. You have almost certainly never in your lives heard anything like this before.'

He picked up his heavy ebony ruler. His little piglike eyes gleamed.

'And,' he went on, 'to make sure that Professor Smallpox will really give us of his best I shall make it my personal business to give Professor Smallpox a clonk on the conk with this tiny weapon should any of you see even the faintest movement of the facial muscles as he delivers his unforgettable message.'

Bill brought down the ruler with a sharp crack on my skull.

'Professor,' he said, 'it's all yours.'

I don't have to go into the next twenty-five minutes. The other boys yelled practically on every syllable. I got the meaningless words tangled up, and said 'A cack of rutter noulded into the gake of a shote.'

At times Bill was so helpless with laughter that he missed me with the ruler altogether.

When the bell went for the end of the hour he insisted on being helped out into the passage, wiping his eyes with the blackboard cloth.

After that, I gave it up, feeling no recurrence of interest even after reading Bill's observation on my end of term report. 'He ought to do well on the stage.'

Patrick Campbell

Security check

It is often said in our age of assembly lines and mass production that there's no room for the individual craftsman, the artist in wood or metal who made so many of the treasures of the past. Like most generalisations, this simply isn't true. He's rarer now, of course, but he's certainly not extinct. He has often had to change his vocation, but in his modest way he still flourishes. Even on the island of Manhatten he may be found, if you know where to look for him. Where rents are low and fire regulations unheard of, his minute, cluttered workshops may be discovered in the basements of apartment houses or in the upper storeys of derelict shops. He may no longer make violins or cuckoo clocks or music boxes, but the skills he uses are the same as they always were, and no two objects he creates are ever identical. He is not contemptuous of mechanisation: you will find several electric hand tools under the debris on his bench. He has moved with the times: he will always be around, the universal odd-job man who is never aware of it when he makes an immortal work of art.

Hans Muller's workshop consisted of a large room at the back of a deserted warehouse, no more than a vigorous stone's throw from the Queensborough Bridge. Most of the building had been boarded up awaiting demolition, and sooner or later Hans would have to move. The only entrance was across a weed-covered yard used as a parking place during the day, and much frequented by the local juvenile delinquents at night. They had never given Hans any trouble, for he knew better than to co-operate with the police when they made their periodic enquiries. The police fully appreciated his delicate position and did not press matters, so Hans was on good terms with everybody. Being a peaceable citizen, that suited him very well.

The work that Hans was now engaged on would have deeply puzzled his Bavarian ancestors. Indeed, ten years ago it would have puzzled Hans himself. And it had all started because a bankrupt client had given him a TV set in payment for services rendered...

Hans had accepted the offer reluctantly, not because he was old-fashioned and disapproved of TV, but simply because he couldn't imagine where he could find time to look at the darned thing. Still, he thought, at least I can always sell it for fifty dollars. But before I do that, let's see what the programmes are like...

His hand had gone out to the switch: the screen had filled with moving shapes – and, like millions of men before him, Hans was lost. He entered a world he had not known existed – a world of battling spaceships, of exotic planets and strange races – the world, in fact of Captain Zipp, Commander of the Space Legion.

Only when the tedious recital of the virtues of Crunche, the Wonder Cereal, had given way to an almost equally tedious boxing match between two muscle-bound characters who seemed to have signed a

non-aggression pact, did the magic fade. Hans was a simple man. He had always been fond of fairy tales – and this was the modern fairy tale, with trimmings of which the Grimm Brothers had never dreamed. So Hans did not sell his TV set.

It was some weeks before the initial naïve, uncritical enjoyment wore off. The first thing that began to annoy Hans was the furniture and general decor of the world of the future. He was, as has been indicated, an artist – and he refused to believe that in a hundred years taste would have deteriorated as badly as the Crunche sponsors seemed to imagine.

He also thought very little of the weapons that Captain Zipp and his opponents used. It was true that Hans did not pretend to understand the principles upon which the portable proton disintegrator was based, but however it worked, there was certainly no reason why it should be that clumsy. The clothes, the spaceship interiors – they just weren't convincing. How did he know? He had always possessed a highly developed sense of the fitness of things, and it could still operate even in this novel field.

We have said that Hans was a simple man. He was also a shrewd one, and he had heard that there was money in TV.

So he sat down and began to draw.

Even if the producer of *Captain Zipp* had not lost patience with his set designer, Hans Muller's ideas would certainly have made him sit up and take notice. There was an authenticity and realism about them that made them quite outstanding. They were completely free from the element of phoneyness that had begun to upset even *Captain Zipp's* most juvenile followers. Hans was hired on the spot.

32

He made his own conditions, however. What he was doing he did largely for love, notwithstanding the fact that it was earning him more money than anything he had ever done in his life. He would take no assistants, and would remain in his little workshop. All that he wanted to do was to produce the prototypes, the basic designs. The mass production could be done somewhere else – he was a craftsman, not a factory.

The arrangement had worked well. Over the last six months *Captain Zipp* had been transformed and was now the despair of all the rival space operators. This, his viewers thought, was not just a serial about the future. It was the future – there was no argument about it. Even the actors seemed to have been inspired by their new surroundings: off the set, they sometimes behaved like twentieth-century time travellers stranded in the Victorian Age, indignant because they no longer had access to the gadgets that had always been part of their lives.

But Hans knew nothing about this. He toiled away happily, refusing to see anyone except the producer, doing all his business over the telephone – and watching the final result to ensure that his ideas had not been mutilated. The only sign of his connection with the slightly fantastic world of commercial TV was a crate of Crunche in one corner of the workshop. He had sampled one mouthful of this present from the grateful sponsor and had then remembered thankfully that, after all, he was not paid to eat the stuff.

He was working late one Sunday evening, putting the final touches to a new design for a space helmet, when he suddenly realised that he was no longer alone.

Slowly he turned from the workbench and faced the door. It had been locked – how could it have been opened so silently? There were two men standing beside it, motionless, watching him. Hans felt his heart trying to climb into his gullet, and summoned up what courage he could to challenge them. At least, he felt thankful, he had little money here. Then he wondered if, after all, this was a good thing. They might be annoyed...

'Who are you?' he asked. 'What are you doing here?'

One of the men moved towards him while the other remained watching alertly from the door. They were both wearing very new overcoats, with hats low down on their heads so that Hans could not see their faces. They were too well dressed, he decided, to be ordinary hold-up men.

'There's no need to be alarmed, Mr Muller,' replied the nearer man, reading his thoughts without difficulty. 'This isn't a hold-up. It's official. We're from – Security.'

'I don't understand.'

The other man reached into a portfolio he had been carrying beneath his coat, and pulled out a sheaf of photographs. He riffled through them until he had found the one he wanted.

'You've given us quite a headache, Mr Muller. It's taken us two weeks to find you – your employers were so secretive. No doubt they

were anxious to hide you from their rivals. However, here we are and I'd like you to answer some questions.'

'I'm not a spy!' answered Hans indignantly as the meaning of the words penetrated. 'You can't do this! I'm a loyal American citizen!'

The other ignored the outburst. He handed over the photograph.

'Do you recognise this?' he said.

'Yes. It's the inside of Captain Zipp's spaceship.'

'And you designed it?'

'Yes.'

Another photograph came out of the file.

'And what about this?'

'That's the Martian city of Paldar, as seen from the air.'

'Your own idea?'

'Certainly,' Hans replied, now too indignant to be cautious.

'And this?'

'Oh, the proton gun. I was quite proud of that.'

'Tell me, Mr Muller – are these all your own ideas?'

'Yes, I don't steal from other people.'

His questioner turned to his companion and spoke for a few minutes in a voice too low for Hans to hear. They seemed to reach agreement on some point, and the conference was over before Hans could make his intended grab at the telephone.

'I'm sorry,' continued the intruder. 'But there has been a serious leak. It may be – uh – accidental, even unconscious, but that does not affect the issue. We will have to investigate you. Please come with us.'

34

There was such power and authority in the stranger's voice that Hans began to climb into his overcoat without a murmur. Somehow, he no longer doubted his visitor's credentials and never thought of asking for any proof. He was worried, but not yet seriously alarmed. Of course, it was obvious what had happened. He remembered hearing about a science-fiction writer during the war who had described the atom bomb with disconcerting accuracy. When so much secret research was going on, such accidents were bound to occur. He wondered just what it was he had given away.

At the doorway, he looked back into his workshop and at the men who were following him.

'It's all a ridiculous mistake,' he said. 'If I did show anything secret in the programme, it was just a coincidence. I've never done anything to annoy the FBI.'

It was then that the second man spoke at last, in very bad English and with a most peculiar accent.

'What is the FBI?' he asked.

But Hans didn't hear him.

He had just seen the spaceship.

Arthur C. Clarke

35

The moonpath

If the world were flat, and if you could look straight into the rising sun, you would see the land where Nick and Bruin lived. It was a land of sticky days and breathless nights, where the sun came up like an enemy and the wind had flies in it.

At the edge of this land where bitter waves met hot sand, there lay a town of flat, ugly buildings and narrow streets and in one of these streets stood a blacksmith's forge.

Nick was apprenticed to the blacksmith. All day in his stiff leather apron he worked by the stinging-hot furnace; pumping the bellows or carrying bars of iron for his master. At night he lay on the dusty floor with a chain on his foot. Nick's mother and father had sold him to the blacksmith for seven years. Nick cried for them sometimes, in the night, but he hated them too, and vowed they would never see him again.

Sometimes Nick's master loaded the things he had made on to a handcart, and Nick pulled it through the town to the customers' homes. As he went along, Nick would search the faces of the people he passed. He always hoped for a smile, or a kindly word, but he never found one. It was a mean, ugly town full of mean, ugly people.

One afternoon as he was hauling the cart across town he saw that a small crowd had gathered in the square. There were shouts, and some laughter. Nick left the cart and went over to look. He was small and thin, and easily slipped through to the front. In the middle of the crowd, on a small patch of beaten dust, stood a bear. There was a collar round its neck with a chain. A man held the chain in one hand and a stick in the other. As Nick watched, the man poked the bear with the stick and cried, 'Down, Bruin!' The bear's legs collapsed and it rolled over in the dust and lay still, playing dead. The people laughed. Somebody dropped a coin in the man's hat. 'Up, Bruin!' cried the man, and he jerked on the chain. The bear clambered slowly to its feet. Nick wondered what it felt like to have a coat of thick fur on such a day as this.

The man jabbed his stick into the bear's side. 'Dance, Bruin!' he snarled.

The bear lifted its forepaws and began a slow shuffle on its hind feet, swinging its great head from side to side.

'Faster!' cried the man, and he struck the creature across its paws.

The people laughed. Bruin tried to move a little faster. There was a cloud of flies round its head; they settled near its eyes.

The man put down the stick and produced a battered mouth-organ. He sucked and blew a scratchy tune, and a few more coins fell into the hat. Bruin moved heavily to the thin music. After a while the man stopped playing and the bear dropped on to all four feet. People clapped a little. The man bowed and grinned. Nick was turning sadly away when the bear raised its head and looked at him. The boy paused, gazing back

into those tiny, pain-filled eyes. In that instant, Nick felt something that
made his own eyes brim, and caused him to clamp his teeth into his
bottom lip. He turned and began to push his way through the crowd. He
felt the bear's eyes following him and could scarcely see through the
tears in his own. He lifted the handles of his cart and went on without
looking back.

That night, lying on the dusty floor with the chain on his foot, Nick
thought about Bruin. He saw the fly-tortured eyes and the dry, lolling
tongue and he murmured softly into the dark, 'Some day, Bruin, we will
leave this place, you and I. We will sail away to a land that is white and
cold as the moon. There will be no flies there, and no chains.' He
moved a little and his chain made a clinking sound. He sighed, and
closed his eyes. 'One day,' he murmured, and then he slept, while the
cold white moon slid silent down the sky.

The next morning his master said, 'Take this boat-hook to Caspar, the
fisherman. You will find him on the sand, mending his nets.'

When he stepped out of the forge the sun hit him and he screwed up
his eyes. 'This land is an anvil,' he told himself. 'The sun is a great
hammer, and it will beat me on the anvil until I am bent and blackened
like the end of this boat-hook.' He wiped the sweat from his forehead
and turned towards the sea.

Caspar was sitting cross-legged in the sand, mending a net. He looked
up, squinting into the sun. 'Ah, my new boat-hook is ready, yes? Give it
here.'

Nick handed it to him and stood wiggling his toes in the hot sand.

The fisherman examined the boat-hook and said, 'Tell your master I am satisfied and will pay him tomorrow.'

Nick bobbed his head, and was turning away when the man said, 'I saw you, yesterday. Watching the bear.'

Nick turned. Pale blue eyes regarding him, a twinkle in them somewhere. He nodded. 'Yes. We are both slaves, the bear and I.'

He knew he ought not to have said it. Suppose the man told his master? His eyes, fearful, met Caspar's. The twinkle remained.

'Have no fear,' said the fisherman softly. 'I have no master, but if I had, it would have been the moonpath for me, long ago.'

Nick did not understand. 'The – moonpath?' he whispered.

Caspar nodded.

'What is the moonpath?' asked Nick. Perhaps this man was mocking him.

The fisherman raised his eyebrows. 'The moonpath? Why, the moonpath is the road to freedom; a silver track that lies upon the sea.'

Nick turned, to see warm, brown water moving slug-like in the sun. His lip twisted up. 'I see no silver track,' he said.

Caspar grinned, shaking his head. 'It is not there now, little slave,' he said. His face became grave and he patted the sand beside him. 'Come, sit here and I will tell you.'

Nick approached the man, half-fearful, and sat down. Caspar set aside his net, drew up his knees under his chin, and wrapped his thick arms around them. He gazed out over the sea.

'It is big, the sea,' he said. 'It is the biggest thing on earth, and the fiercest. To cross it you need a good boat.' He glanced sidelong at Nick. 'Slaves do not have boats. But sometimes at night, in the full of the moon, there is a way for them if they believe and are brave.'

Nick waited. After a moment, Caspar nodded towards the sea, 'Out there' he said, 'When the moon is full, there is a path across the sea. It is long and straight, and at the far end lies a land as cool as this land is hot.' He turned earnest eyes to Nick. 'He who takes the silver path must travel quickly, for it melts with the dawn and is no more until the moon is full again.'

The boy felt a lump in his throat and he gazed at Caspar through tear-filled eyes. 'I have seen such a path,' he choked. 'It is made from light. No one can walk upon it. You mock me.'

Caspar shrugged. 'I told you. A man must believe, and be brave.' He took up a net and began to work upon it as though Nick were no longer there.

After a while the boy blinked away his tears, got up, and walked towards the town.

Many days passed. One evening, at the end of a very hard day, Nick's master beat him and left him waterless. Nick lay a long time crying in the dust. When he had cried all his tears, he sat up and rubbed his eyes with the heels of his hands so that the dust from them made a grey paste on his cheeks.

'I will not stay here,' he told himself, 'to be beaten and starved and roasted. I will run away. I will go tonight.' And he crawled across the floor to where his master had left a large file. His chain was barely long enough, but by lying at full stretch he was able to get his finger-tips to it. He laid the blade across a link and, working rapidly, began to saw at the iron.

An hour he worked, then rested, gasping. He blinked away the sweat and went on. At midnight the link parted. Nick scrambled to his feet and stood, listening. The moon-washed streets were silent.

He left the forge on tiptoe, flitting from shadow to shadow along the road. He did not know where he would go. The town was surrounded on three sides by the desert, and on the other by the sea. The desert, then. He must try to cross the desert. He turned up an alley, and cried out in terror. His master came swiftly, crouching, the great hammer drawn back over a brawny shoulder. Nick whirled and fled.

'Runaway!' roared his master behind him.

His voice echoed all across the midnight town. A door was flung open. Then another. Lights moved in windows. People spilled out of houses. Nick swerved and ran on. The people were shouting to one another. His way was blocked. He spun round. Men, strung out across the street behind him, and his master like some squat ape coming with the hammer. He ran left. A figure crouched, spreading huge arms. He spun. There! A clear run. He gasped, pelting along the unguarded alley, and as he ran he cried out, without knowing it, the name of the only other slave he knew. 'Bruin! Bruin! Bruin!...'

Breaking clear of the buildings he glanced over his shoulder. His master followed, closer now, his hammer raised high. Nick ran on desperately then stopped, skidding in damp sand. The sea! They had driven him to the sea! He turned, sobbing, and angled along the beach, dodging between huge rocks and leaping over small ones. He could hear the pounding of his master's boots and the rasping of his breath. He threw back his head and ran wild-eyed, mouth agape. He never saw the rock. It struck him below the knees and he went headlong in the sand. He rolled and screamed, flinging up his arms to cover his face. His master raised the great hammer. A cry. The hammer fell, kicking up sand by Nick's head, and then his master reeled, clutching his side.

A shaggy form swayed erect against the moon, snarling. Bruin! The bear turned, a short length of chain swinging at its neck. Nick gazed up at the great head and then beyond, to where the moon hung cool and full in the velvet sky. Cool and full. Caspar! The boy looked seaward, and it was there. 'I believe!' sobbed Nick.

Men were coming, running quiet in the sand. He scrambled to his feet. 'Come, Bruin!' he cried.

The sand sloped gently down, and they ran; not into surf, but on to rippled silver, cool and hard. 'I believe!' cried Nick, and they moved out across the midnight sea.

And all along the shore the people stood, their mouths open, staring. One stuck out his foot and snatched it back, drenched with moon-white spray. So they stood, all night, gazing out to sea. From time to time someone would shake his head, or mutter something under his breath. And when it was near to dawn, they looked at one another out of the corners of their eyes, and shuffled their feet, and began to drift away in ones and twos. They walked by the blacksmith, who nursed his side by a rock. And the blacksmith said to one, 'Where is my boy?' and to another, 'What happened?' But they just shook their heads like people in a dream.

And then the bear's master came dangling the broken lock from Bruin's cage. Far, far away, a cooling wind ruffled Nick's hair and Bruin dropped his head to lap the snow.

Robert Swindells

Noulded into the shake of a goat

Thinking about the story

1 What sort of person is Bill the Bull, do you think?
2 How do we know that the other pupils were enjoying Patrick's embarrassment?
3 Look again at the author's description of himself in the first sentence. If this is true, what do you think of the teacher's treatment of him?

Problems with labials

'Labials' are sounds which require you to move or close your lips. For example the first sound in the word 'bat'. They are very difficult for a ventriloquist to master, because he/she must not move the lips at all.

1 Make a list of as many single sounds as you can think of that require you to move your lips. (The easiest ways to do this are to use a mirror, or to work with a partner.)
2 Make up a list of words that contain these sounds.
3 Try to say the words in your list without moving your lips.
4 Try the phrases mentioned by Dr Farvox in his book.

Writing

How do you think Bill the Bull felt when he got back to the staff-room after the lesson? How did he describe the lesson to the other teachers? Write his version of events.

Security check

Thinking about the story

1 Why had Hans not had a television set before?
2 What two things about television made the 'magic fade' for Hans?
3 Why had Hans' ideas come at just the right time for the producer of *Captain Zipp*?
4 Is there anything about the visitors which should have made Hans (and the reader) suspicious before the last sentence of the story?

The shape of the story

There are some 'time-leaps' in this story. We have to assume that certain things have happened. Work out what happened:
1 Between 'So he sat down and began to draw' and 'Even if the producer ...'
2 Between 'he was a craftsman and not a factory' and 'The arrangement worked well'.

Writing

'His questioner turned to his companion and spoke for a few minutes ...' Think about what they may have said to each other.
1 Make a list of the main things that you think were said.
2 Suppose that you are one of the two visitors. When you get back to base you have to report what you did and what happened.
   Write the part of the report that describes this conversation.

The moonpath

Thinking about the story

1 From the first three paragraphs, make two lists of words and phrases: one list describing the place, and the other list describing the weather.
2 Are you surprised at the last sentence of paragraph four? Why does the author repeat 'mean' and 'ugly', do you think?
3 Why is Nick in tears when he sees the bear for the first time?
4 How different is Caspar, the fisherman, from other people in the town?
5 Why does Caspar tell Nick the story of the moonpath?
6 What finally drove Nick to try to escape?
7 Some writers use short sentences to show that things are happening quickly, and/or to show that thoughts are flashing through a character's mind. Give some examples from this story of where the author uses short sentences for these purposes.

Writing

1 What do you think Nick's thoughts would be when they reached the safety of the faraway land? What was it like? Write as if you were Nick.
2 Imagine that you are Bruin. Write 'My story' from the moment you first see Nick.

If only ...

Thinking and talking

You have read three stories, and at the end of each you might have thought 'If only...'

1 If only Patrick Campbell had been a successful ventriloquist at school ...
2 If only we could see into the future ...
3 If only we could really achieve what we wanted by having faith in ourselves ...

Suppose that these things can happen; suppose that one of them has happened to you. Discuss:

1 Which one you would choose and why.
2 What it would be like.
3 How other people would react.
4 How you would feel about it.

Writing

Now tell other people in the class about your ideas. Do it by writing a story about 'The day I...' (Finish the title yourself.)

Soap Street

Hi there. Welcome to Soap Street. Not much of a street really. Not much different to any other street I don't suppose. My name's Josie by the way, Josie Robinson. My dad Cliff owns the shop there on the corner, the Sunshine Store. He came from Jamaica when he was a boy, then met my mum Tilly, and they built up the business together. I've an elder brother Lenny who's in his last year at school. He plays in a band with some lads in the Street. They're not bad, but I wouldn't tell him that! So you see, a pretty ordinary family really.

I'm just off on my morning paper round. I don't mind getting up early before everyone else is awake. I like to see the Street coming to life. It's amazing the things you get to know about people just by delivering their papers, or when they come in to the shop for a few bits and pieces. The gossip kind of gets mixed up with the groceries and veg and carried up and down the street with the shopping. So there's not much I don't know about the things that go on. Just ordinary things I know, but kinda interesting. If you come along on my round. I'll tell you a bit about them...

Josie

43

mum & Dad

Me!

Tony & Maggie

Here's the Sunshine Store. There's not much sunshine at the moment though. Dad comes in the other evening looking mad as hell. Kids spraying things on the shop again, you know the kind of thing. He tells us he's sick of things here, wants to sell the shop and go back to Jamaica. We were all stunned for a moment, then everyone joined in. What about Lenny's band, selling the shop, leaving our friends, what'd we do in Jamaica? 'My mind's made up!' says Cliff storming out. So who knows what'll happen...

Next door's the 'Jack O'Lantern'. Maggie runs the place while Tony thinks up bright ideas to boost trade. His latest scheme is to run a talent contest. He only wants a chance to do his Elvis impersonation (again!). But when Maggie found out he was going to have a beauty contest as well she put her foot down, and has got up a women's football team to challenge the men instead. I'm playing, so it should be good for a laugh! Just as long as Tony doesn't try to hold the beauty contest anyway...

Meet Scott, my ex-boyfriend since the row we had last week. I still like him a lot, but when he said we could make some money starting a baby-sitting business, I should have left him to get on with it on his own. Being stupid I gave him a hand minding the Johnsons' kids. I was lucky to escape those brats alive! Haven't spoken to Scott since. I must tell you the whole story sometime...

Betty Parkes lives at Number 4. She's been engaged to Arthur Bunt next door for seven years, but hasn't named the day yet. 'Marry in haste, repent at leisure', says Betty. 'Any day now,' says Arthur with a sly wink. 'I've a little plan that'll help her to make up her mind...'

Here's Rachel Crouch, poking her nose into everyone's business. I dread to see her coming into the shop, always complaining. The noise from the pub, the smell of the animals at the Cartwrights' place, the kids in the street. Nothing suits her. One of these days, someone is going to give her a piece of their mind...

Scott

Betty Parkes

Arthur Bunt

Rachel Crouch

Des   George Sharpe   Chai   Wang Lo

Meet George Sharpe. But watch your wallet. George sells cars, guaranteed – to go wrong! Desmond works for him as mechanic, dogsbody, and general handyman. If there's a dirty job to be done, George disappears and leaves Des in the lurch. Take the other day. Des sold a car to Inspector Boulder down at the nick. 'You've done what?!' said George, letting his cigar drop from his mouth. 'Not the blue Escort?' 'Yes,' said Des really pleased, 'Good eh?' 'Not good,' said George, 'not good at all...' I wonder why?

George Sharpe sold Wang Lo his first motor bike. It bust of course, but Wang soon got it going again. I wish he hadn't, because he's had one accident already. Bust a rib or two and smashed his helmet. His parents are worried sick about him. So is his sister Chai. She gets really fed up having to mind her young brother and sister while her parents work in the Takeaway, or serve behind the counter herself. 'The teachers are all complaining I'm not doing my work but I'm tired out,' she says. 'It's just not fair!'

Over the road lives Sara Harris. Her brother Brian's seventeen, and always in trouble, fighting or pinching things. Trouble is, he gets Sara to cover up for him. 'One of these days,' she says, 'he'll ask one favour too many...' He's been very pally with George Sharpe just lately too...

Here's the Johnsons, where Scott got us that baby-sitting job looking after their little terrors, aged two, three, four. Terry is a DIY freak. You can be having a quiet chat with his wife Ruby, when he suddenly leaps in with a hammer and

starts knocking holes in the walls. And he's totally useless! 'That's it,' says Ruby one day, 'I'll fix the house up, you mind the kids!' She plonks the baby in his lap, and goes off with his drill...

Poor Joey Snow lives in the end house. He's got a rotten life. His mother's gone off, and his dad doesn't care. He comes in to the shop every morning buying crisps for his breakfast. Only time he ever smiles is when he's next door at the Cartwrights' messing about with their animals. The thing is, Joey's gone missing...

Brian & Sara Harris   Ruby & Terry Johnson   Joey Snow

Rosie Gilbert runs a boarding house, a real character, with a tremendous laugh, and a temper to match. She used to be a singer and dancer, keeps an album of all her press cuttings. She'll show you if you ask her. Lots of her boarders are theatrical types. The other boys in Lenny's band are dodging Rosie for the rent they owe. Then there's the 'Great Hypno', a magician. A bit too fond of a drink so Rosie tells me. Like the night when down at the 'Lantern' he hypnotised loads of the regulars into doing daft things. I just wish that I'd seen it...

Inspector Boulder runs the local Police Station, keeping an eye on the street. He looks very fierce, an ex-police boxing champion, so I wouldn't want to get on the wrong side of him. WPC Kettle has just joined. She comes down to the youth club with PC Davies to teach us self-defence. It was great when she threw him right over her shoulder. Scott had better watch out! We're thinking of ways to make some cash to buy a few things for the Youth Club. Any ideas?

Ken and Sheila Cartwright keep a kind of zoo-farm for any animal which has been lost, hurt or ill-treated. Perhaps that's why Joey spends so much time there. Rachel Crouch and the Jenkins next door are always writing letters to the paper or the council to complain. 'What if the animals escape?' 'Danger to health', you know the sort of thing. 'We may have to get rid of them,' Sheila said. 'Perhaps that's got something to do with Joey disappearing... Especially as the chimp's gone too!'...

Claire Jenkins is a gas, a bundle of laughs. Her parents are a bit stuck up though. Claire really likes the animals, and says she'll hide them in her house if she has to! Her parents are in Spain at the moment, having a miserable time. Claire showed me their postcard. 'Hotel awful. Food terrible. Weather stormy. Wish you were here.' She's planned a big party for Saturday night, the whole street's been invited. Lenny and the band are doing the music... Just as long as her parents don't decide to come home early...

Miss Howard's

Rev. Mathews

Miss Howard lives in the gloomy old house at the end of the road. No one has ever seen her except her old housekeeper, who keeps her lips as tight as her purse and says nothing. The garden's overgrown, with high railings all round. Kids play there, hiding in the bushes, telling stories about getting caught, and wondering why she is never seen. Only one kid, Gary, has ever been inside the house. And when he got out, he ran straight off home, and never would say what he found inside...

The Rev. Matthews runs the church and the youth club next door. When some of the kids start getting out of hand, he gets Inspector Boulder to give the lads a few boxing lessons. They soon settle down! You have to go through the dark church yard to get to the club in the hall at the back. One night I saw something. I ran down the path to get to the light of the door as quick as I could, feeling cold like electric all over my skin. The Rev. Matthews took one look at my face. 'You've seen it too!' he said...

Another of my friends is going through a rough time at the moment. Zena came into school one day and burst into tears in the middle of a lesson. The teacher asked me to look after her and eventually Zena told me the reason. Her parents are getting divorced. I just couldn't believe it. I mean everyone's parents have rows, but you never think they'll leave each other because of it. She's got a younger brother, Alan, and he was really upset. Poor Zena. How will she choose who to live with...?

My best friend, Usha, has been going out with Brian Harris. I just don't know what she sees in him. And I tell her so, me with my big mouth. She says he's not like people think, there's a side to him other people don't see. 'He keeps it well hidden,' I say, tactful as ever. Her parents don't know, of course, and they're pretty strict, don't want to see her get hurt. But Usha can't see that. She's been inventing all sorts of excuses to get out to see Brian. What I do know is, there'll be some explaining to do, whey they find out...

Zena's Parents

Usha

Usha's Parents

Home base

When you've read about the people in Soap Street, compare them with people who live near you.

Draw a large map of your neighbourhood. Label the names of the roads, number the houses, and show where people live. Put in the shops, the doctor's surgery, the police station and so on.

Taking off

Now make up a Street of your own. Either continue Soap Street by adding more characters who are based on people you know or invent a completely new neighbourhood. Set your work out in the same way as Soap Street. Draw the houses and the people who live there, then write a short description of them. Think about these points:

1 What do they look like?
2 Who else is in their family?
3 How old are they?
4 What do they do?
5 How do they get on with other people?
6 What do other people in the street think or say about them?
7 What problems do they have?
8 What has happened to them that might be interesting to other people?

If you work with a group of people, your houses and people can be joined together to form a complete street.

Write a play script

Choose whichever of the characters and families from Soap Street you find most interesting. Think about what they might say to each other when they discuss their problems. (For example, what might Tilly, Lenny and Josie say to Cliff when he breaks the news to them that he wants to return to live in Jamaica?)

Write out the conversations which take place. If you are not sure how to set the script out, look on page 180.

Make up a local newspaper

Use the information Josie gives you about the people in the street to write an edition of the local paper *The Soap Street News*. You will need to include all the different articles and items which newspapers usually have, and lay out the pages in columns with headlines, photographs, and illustrations. Here are some ideas for headlines.

Joey Snow missing . . .

Local animal refuge to close

Boy injured in motor bike crash

Hypnotist put regulars in a trance

Local party noise causes complaints

Car trader accused

Write a story

Each of the situations Josie describes can be developed into a story:

1 Read what she says and look for the clues she gives to suggest how the story goes on.
2 Think about what could happen next. Is there more than one possible development? If so make a list or flow chart to examine the possibilities. Choose the one that looks most interesting.
3 Decide where the events of the story take place.
4 Make a list of the scenes in the story, showing where and when they take place and what happens.
5 Think about the characters. How will they react to the events in the story?
6 Think about how people will speak and include some conversations in your story.
7 Decide who will tell the story. (What difference will this make to the way it is told?)

The Robinson affair

Mr Robinson was sitting on our front door-step the day we moved in. He was young and handsome and friendly. The children took to him straight away. He was helpful, too, making numerous journeys to and from the van to ensure that everything was being handled correctly. We were delighted when he stayed for lunch but as supper-time approached we began to feel a bit awkward. It would seem ungracious to ask him to leave after all his kindness, but we'd had a long day and wanted to get to bed. We left the door open. He went out. He came back. During the next few days we made all the right sort of enquiries. We even advertised in the local press but no-one came forward. By the end of the week he had become part of the household and we were the proud owners of a delightful marmalade cat.

It must have been five years later that my wife's sister went to America, from the April to the September. There was no-one to mind her budgerigar. We took him – with reservations. The first couple of months were uneventful. Joey settled in straight away. He didn't talk but he seemed happy enough swinging gently on his perch, turning an occasional somersault. Mr Robinson would sit perfectly still and watch him from the other side of the room. He never went near the cage. I walked up from the station one evening in early June. My wife and Mr Robinson met me at the gate. She was a bit concerned. 'We'll have to watch Mr Robinson with that bird.' I was looking at the greenfly on the

Wendy Cussons. 'What happened?' 'Well, Joey started to chatter a bit after lunch and this fellow –' she scooped Mr Robinson up in her arms – 'was on the settee in a flash.' We had a look in the living room. The cage was a bit near the settee but it was fairly high up and there really was no-where else to put it. We watched Mr Robinson's dignified progress down the garden. We would have to be vigilant.

As time went on, Joey became bolder. His two months of silence had not been wasted. He had been listening and building up a repertoire. His mimicry was brilliant and revealing. None of us escaped. He took the greatest pleasure in tormenting Mr Robinson. From the safety of his eyrie he would hurl abuse while turning frantic somersaults or he would swing slowly backwards and forwards mocking him in a gentle little voice. This was even more infuriating. All the while Mr Robinson behaved perfectly. He kept to his side of the room and watched, sphinx-like and silent.

There were new neighbours next door. We'd had to go out in the morning and by the time we got back they had moved in. It was a lovely September day and to welcome them we all had lunch in the garden. I'd just gone into the house for something when there was a commotion outside. Mr Robinson leapt in through the open window carrying a squawking bird in his mouth, hotly pursued by my wife and the new

neighbours. The clamour was incredible. He ran along the back of the settee, put his paw up to the door of the cage then stood, transfixed. Joey was sitting quietly on his perch peering down disapprovingly at these goings-on.

Mr Robinson's jaw dropped in astonishment. I caught the bird as it fell. It was completely unharmed. I tried to explain, 'You see our old neighbours didn't have a bird and when Mr Robinson saw yours he thought you had stolen ours.'

My sister-in-law collected Joey the following week-end. Mr Robinson sat on the gate-post and watched them go. It had been a bit of a dog's life but he would miss him. Life might even become a bit dull. He walked around the side of the house and paused meditatively at the gap in our neighbour's fence. There was this new chap next door.

Joan Brookman

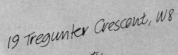

19 Tregunter Crescent, W8

Your Majesty,

After much hesitation I am taking the liberty of writing to you to ask a favour on behalf of my daughter, Penelope. Young Penny, a well developed 12 year old, has recently 'taken up' tennis and has visions of becoming a second Christine Truman! There are no courts at her Comprehensive, though promised, and she 'makes do' in the park. On my way to and from work (at the Army and Navy Stores) my bus takes me between Victoria and Hyde Park Corner and past the Palace gardens. These have always intrigued me and from the top of the bus one gets a lovely view. With the leaves off the trees, your hard tennis court becomes very clear. It looks in perfect condition, with everything ready and the net up, but I have never seen anyone playing on it. Would it be possible, I wonder, for my Penny to make use of it?

Yours sincerely,
Pamela Johnston

From the Lady Jean Sidebotham
Buckingham Palace, SW1

Dear Mrs Johnston,

Her Majesty has commanded me to answer your letter and to say that she regrets that she does not feel able at the present time to agree to your request.

Yours sincerely,

Jean Sidebotham

Jean Sidebotham
Lady-in-Waiting to Her Majesty

Dear Lady Sidebotham,

There seems to have been some misunderstanding. I was not expecting that Her Majesty would be able to play with Penny, she is clearly much too busy.

My daughter would bring along one of her friends. Of course, if Her Majesty would care for a knock-up during a slack time in state affairs, that would be a marvellous bonus!

Penny and her friend would bring their own tennis balls. Their best days would be Tuesday or Friday about 2:30pm. They are both very excited at the possibility.

Yours Sincerely,

Pamela Johnston

— —

Dear Mrs Johnston,
Your further letter has been considered and it is regretted that no exception can be made in this case.
Yours sincerely,

Jean Sidebotham

Jean Sidebotham

20 Tregunter Crescent, W8

Dear Queen,

My good friend and neighbour, Mrs Johnston, has been telling me how you are planning to be throwing open your tennis courts to youngsters. This is being great good news. My daughter, Helga, 'caught the tennis bug' while staying with her Onkel Heinrich in Hanover last summer and would also like to 'join up' with the group.

Hullo!

Gertrud Bauscher

Dear Mrs Bauscher,
Her Majesty has commanded me to answer your letter and to say that she is sorry that you have been misinformed and that the tennis court cannot be liberated for public use.
Yours sincerely,

Jean Sidebotham

Jean Sidebotham

Dear Lady Sidebotham,
I understand that Mrs Bauscher has written - it was foolish of me to let her into our little secret. Of course, if you extend the invitation to everybody the court would become impossibly overcrowded and this is the last thing we want. When would it be convenient for the children to play?
Yours Sincerely
Pamela Johnston

Dear Mrs Johnston,
I would very much like to be more helpful but it will be clear to you that the question of security is, in these sad days, of paramount importance and this, if for no other reason, prevents us giving your daughter access to the Palace grounds.
Yours sincerely,
Jean Sidebotham
Jean Sidebotham

Dear Lady Sidebotham,
You need have no fear about security. Penny knows better than to damage any trees or shrubs in the garden. We have always brought her up to respect other people's property. Did I spot a side-door to the Palace which the children could use? It's in that wall near to where dear old Gorringes used to be. If the children were to use that there would be less chance of outsiders getting to know what was going on. They would be careful to stick to the path once inside the Palace grounds. What about next Friday?
Yours Sincerely,
Pamela Johnston

Dear Lady Sidebottom,
I am not understanding why Helga's tickets for the court have not come through. Penny Johnston is cock-a-hop all over the Crescent and nothing for Helga! Is this being British Justice? Hullo!
Gertrud Bauscher

Dear Mrs Bauscher,
I am afraid that you are under a misapprehension. No tickets are being issued to anybody for Her Majesty's hard tennis court. The question of security is, these sad days, of paramount importance.
Yours sincerely,
Jean Sidebotham
Jean Sidebotham

Dear Lady Sidebottom.

We Germans are not fearful persons. We mind little of security. A true German is as secure on tennis-court as on battle-field. Helga fears nothing. She has her karate medal and can protect herself.

Hullo!
Gertrud Bauscher

Dear Lady Sidebotham,

I wonder if you can have received my last letter. The children are 'all set'—and no news! Next week will be half term and an ideal moment for the children's first visit. Please let me know soon.

Yours sincerely.
Pamela Johnston

From the Hon. Mrs J.C.B. Tynte
Buckingham Palace, SW1

Dear Mrs Johnston,
Lady Jean is away from duty at the moment with a complete nervous breakdown and in her absence I am dealing with her letters. As the volume of incoming correspondence is always very great, it is not the palace practice to retain many letters from the public, or our answers to them, and so I am in some doubt about the 'first visit' to which you refer. Could you please explain?
Yours sincerely,

Muriel Tynte

Muriel Tynte
Lady-in-Waiting to Her Majesty

Dear Mrs Tynte,
Certainly... My daughter, Penelope, has recently 'taken up' tennis...

54

Arthur Marshall

Mum takes a bath

On a normal, average day in our house:
Tracey and Darren
are fighting with Sharon,
the TV set's blaring,
and Gran's started swearing,
the cat caught his paw
when Michelle slammed the door
and he's rowling and yowling in pain;
once again, baby Shane's
stuck his hand down the drain
and he can't get his thumb out
so he's screaming his lungs out:
the shrill accusations
and reverberations
of the whole pandemonium's mass aggravations
are shaking the house from the roof to
foundations –

I go to the bathroom
and lock myself in.
I go to the bathroom
and shut out the din.
I go to the bathroom and turn on the taps.
And I peel them all off like a skin.
Because
in the water
the warm, silky water
the deep, soothing water
with my ears under water
I can't
hear
a thing...

Mick Gowar

Stubborn husband, stubborn wife

There was a time and there wasn't a time in the long ago when a man and wife lived together in a small house in the city of Hamadan. The wife was industrious and hard-working and was busy from morning till night. The man was lazy and good-for-nothing. They argued and quarrelled all day long.

One day, the wife said, 'It's a disgrace the way you sit all day on the bench in front of the house staring at the sky and doing nothing at all. Are you afraid to move for fear that the wind will blow off your beard?'

The man said, 'What is there for me to do? I inherited a flock of sheep from my father and I gave them to a shepherd. In return, he gives us cheese and milk and wool, and with this we eat and clothe ourselves. You are strong and able to do the cooking and cleaning and washing.' Then the man folded his arms and stared at the sky.

The wife said, 'What about the calf in the stable? Every day I give the calf its water. That is man's work. I will not do it any more. You will have to break a rib, now and then, and water the calf yourself.'

The man said, 'If you can't do a little job like watering the calf, then what are you good for?'

The wife answered, 'I am good for woman's work. I cook for you and sew for you. I wash for you and dry for you. But I will not water the calf.'

The man said, 'That is not right. I brought you to my house to do what I tell you, even if I tell you to throw yourself off the roof. It has been said by the poets that men are the masters of women. Whatever a man orders, a woman must do.'

At these words, the wife grew angry and said, 'Yes, the poets have written those words about real men, brave men, not about donkey droppings like you.'

And so they argued and quarrelled about who would water the calf. At last, they reached an agreement. The wife said she would water the calf that day. But, starting tomorrow, they agreed that whoever spoke the first word in the morning would have to water the calf forever after. If the wife should speak first, she agreed to water the calf without complaining. And if the man should speak first, he agreed to water it.

And so they went to bed, each promising himself that, on the next day, he would refuse to utter a word until the other had spoken.

The next morning, the woman got up early, rolled up her mattress, swept the house, prepared the breakfast, but said nothing. The man, too, got up, put on his clothes, ate his breakfast, and said nothing.

The woman watched angrily as her husband prepared to go out as usual and sit on the bench and stare at the sky. Ten times in ten minutes she wanted to shout at him in anger. At last, she put on her veil and went to the neighbour's house so she would be away from him and couldn't speak to him even if she wanted to.

The man watched his wife as she put on her cloak and left the house
and walked over to the neighbour's house. He wondered what she was
up to, but he did not say a word. After she had gone, he went outside
and sat on the stone bench in front of the house and began to look at the
sky.

Soon a beggar came along. Seeing the man sitting there, the beggar
approached and said, 'In the name of Allah, a piece of bread and a slice
of onion, master, and may your shadow never grow shorter.'

The man said nothing, so the beggar raised his voice and asked again
for a piece of bread or a few pennies. Still the man gave no answer.

'This is strange,' the beggar said to himself. 'This man is moving and
breathing, but he doesn't talk. Maybe he is deaf.' So, the beggar began
to shout.

Still the man said not a word, for he was thinking, 'My wife has sent
this beggar to make me talk. As soon as I open my mouth, she will
come out of the neighbour's house and say, "You spoke first. Hurry up
and water the calf." I won't be taken in by her tricks. If earth flies up to
heaven or if heaven falls down to earth, I will not move my tongue in
my mouth.'

By this time, the beggar saw the man was not going to say anything,
so he walked past the man and went into the house. He filled his
beggar's bowl with all the bread and cheese he could find and then went
away. The man saw all this, but said nothing, because he was afraid that
if he spoke, he would have to water the calf every day.

Soon a travelling barber came walking down the street. When he saw
the man sitting on the bench, he said, 'Do you want me to give your
beard a trim?'

The man said nothing. So, the barber thought to himself, 'If he didn't want me to fix up his hair and trim his beard, he would have spoken up. So, I guess he wants me to work on him.'

The barber began to sharpen his razor against his whetstone and soon he had trimmed the man's beard and cut his hair short. Then the barber held out his hand for payment.

The man said nothing. The barber asked for his money three times, but got no answer. This made him angry. 'Pay me!' he shouted. 'Or I will shave off your beard so you'll look like a woman, and I'll fix your hair to look like a duck's tail.' When the man still didn't answer, the barber flew into a rage. He took out his razor and shaved off the man's beard until the man's face was as smooth as the palm of his hand. And he fixed the man's hair to look like a duck's tail. Then the barber went away.

Soon an old woman came hobbling down the street. She was a seller of paint and powder for ladies. As soon as she saw the man with his face all shaven, she thought he was a woman. She said, 'My lady, why are you sitting here without your veil? And why have you cut your hair so short?'

The man did not answer, so the old woman reached in her knapsack and took out her pots of paint and powder and some false hair besides. 'My lady,' she said, coming closer, 'you will shame your husband sitting here like this with your hair short and without your veil.' The old woman put false hair on the man's head. Then she put rouge on his cheeks and berry juice on his lips and powdered his face all over. When she had finished, she wanted to be paid.

The man said nothing, so the old woman reached in his pocket and took all his money and went away.

58

Now a clever thief came along. He saw what he thought was a woman sitting on the bench in front of the house and he saw the door wide open. He stopped and said in a sweet voice, 'My lady, why have you left your door open? Do you not know that thieves are all around? And why are you sitting outside your house without your veil? Is your husband not at home to keep you safe inside?'

When the thief received no answer, he said to himself, 'This woman is deaf and dumb.' So he said, 'My lady, since your door is open, do you mind if I step inside for a word with your husband?'

The man still said nothing. He was thinking, 'My wife has sent this person to make me open my mouth, just as she sent all the others. I know my wife. She is hiding behind the neighbour's window and listening. As soon as I speak, she will run out and say, "You spoke first. Hurry up and water the calf." But I am not going to give in just because of a few troubles.'

Now the thief saw that whatever he said, not a sound came from the woman sitting on the bench. So, the thief went into the house. When he saw that no one was home, he searched the house and gathered up everything that had a light weight and a heavy price. He put the rugs, the pots and pans, and all the clothing he could find into his satchel and went away.

All this time, the calf in the stable was weak with thirst. The poor calf began to bang its head against the stable door in despair and soon knocked the door down. It ran through the house and out into the street, and began bawling for water.

When the man saw the calf he said to himself, 'That wicked wife of mine has even told the calf to come out and start bawling so that I will be forced to speak. But I haven't answered any of the others and I won't answer the calf, either.'

Just at this moment, the wife looked out of the neighbour's window and saw the calf running away down the street to the stream. She hurried out of the neighbour's house and caught the calf and took it home. As she came to her house, leading the calf, she suddenly saw her husband sitting on the stone bench wearing false hair, with rouge on his cheeks and berry juice on his lips and powder on his face. She did not recognise him and thought to herself, 'That wicked husband of mine has married another wife and brought her here in my place because I refused to water the calf.'

She went over to her husband and said, 'O woman, who told you to come here and sit before my house?'

With a shout of joy, the man jumped up and said, 'You spoke first! Hurry up and water the calf.' Then he took off his false fair and laughed and laughed.

When the woman saw that this strange creature was her husband, with his face shaven and his cheeks painted, she said, 'Dust on your head. Who has done this to you? Who has shaved you?'

She ran into the house in a rage. She saw all the boxes thrown about, the shelves empty, the rugs gone, and she realised that a thief had come

and taken everything. She ran outside again and said to her husband,
'What was the matter with you? Were you dead or sleeping that you
didn't protest?'

The man said, 'I was neither dead nor sleeping, but I knew you told
all those people to come and force me to talk so I would have to water
the calf.'

The woman said, 'Dust on your stubborn head! You lost what you had
and what you'll never have. You lost your face, you lost your money,
you lost your rugs – and all because of your stubbornness. And yet you
are happy because you don't have to water the calf.'

The man smiled and said, 'The wise men have said that when a man
orders, a woman must obey.'

The wife said, 'O stubborn man, you have lost your wife, too. I am
going away and I shall take the calf, since you refuse to water it.' So,
the woman ran off down the street and the calf followed her.

When she came to the edge of town, she asked some children who
were playing, 'Did you see a man with a satchel coming out of my
house?' The children told her that a man with a satchel had passed them
half an hour ago and that he had taken the road across the desert.

The woman took the calf's halter in her hand and started out across
the desert. Soon she saw a man with a satchel walking ahead of her. She
knew he was the thief, so she hurried to catch up with him. She walked
very fast and soon she came up to the thief and passed him.

The thief called, 'Where are you going, sister?'

The woman said in a weak voice, 'O stranger, I am going to my
home.'

'Why do you walk so fast?'

She said, 'I must get to a caravanserai before it is dark, as I am afraid

60

to spend the night alone in the desert with no one to guard me but my calf. If I had someone to protect me, I would walk slower.'

The thief saw that she was very pretty, so he said, 'If you walk slower, we can walk together and I will protect you.'

'I don't mind,' she said, smiling very sweetly at him.

So, the wife and the thief walked on together and the woman began to give him tender glances. 'O stranger,' she said, 'how lucky I was to meet a fine, strong man to protect me and care for me.' And she smiled even more sweetly and gave him a thousand loving glances from her dark eyes.

The thief said to himself, 'She is not bad looking.' Then he asked, 'Lady sister, don't you have a husband?'

She said, 'If I had a husband, would I be all alone in the desert with a calf?'

So, they walked on, and all the time the wife kept sighing and sending loving glances at the thief. Before the afternoon was half over, he asked her to be his wife and she agreed to go with him to the headman in the next town and get married.

Now, the wife did not love the thief at all and certainly did not want to marry a thief. In fact, the farther she got from home, the more she thought of her stubborn husband and her heart burned for him. But she had a plan.

She said to the thief, 'And when we are married, how will you feed me and clothe me?'

The thief said, 'In my satchel there is money enough and clothes enough.'

The woman said, 'Let me see in your satchel.'

But the thief said, 'Not now. You shall see when we are married.'

They walked on until the sun set, when they came to the next village. They went to the headman's house and asked if he could marry them. The headman agreed and promised to marry them in the morning. He gave them supper and prepared a bedroll for the night. 'I have only one guest room,' the headman said. 'Lady, you may sleep this night on the bedroll of my guest room and your beloved will sleep on the floor next to you. Tomorrow, you will be married at dawn, and then you will go on your journey as man and wife.'

So, the wife lay down on the bedroll and the thief stretched out on the floor, and the headman went off to sleep in his own room. Before the thief went to sleep, he placed his satchel next to the door.

Very soon, the thief's snores were so loud they reached the sky. The wife quietly got up and tiptoed to the headman's kitchen. She took a handful of flour and mixed it with water and cooked it over a candle flame until it was paste. Then she poured the paste into the headman's shoes and into the thief's shoes.

Next, she went to get the satchel, but it was too heavy for her to carry, so she dragged it out of the house where she found the calf tied to a post. She put the satchel on the calf's back and started home across the desert just as the sun peeped above the horizon.

At this time, the headman woke up, stretched himself and went to put on his shoes. The paste had hardened and he couldn't get his feet inside. 'I cannot marry my guests without shoes,' he said to himself, 'I wonder what has happened.'

He went to his guests' room in his bare feet and there he found the door open and the woman gone. Only the man remained, sound asleep on the floor. The headman shouted, 'Say, uncle! Where is your bride?'

The thief woke up and saw that the wife was gone and the satchel, too. He jumped up and ran to put on his shoes, but the paste inside them had hardened and he couldn't get his feet inside. Without saying a word to the headman, the thief ran out of the house and down the road to the

desert in his bare feet. He ran as fast as he could, but he had gone no more than a league when he had to stop. His feet were sore and bleeding and he couldn't run a step farther. In a rage, he sat down by the roadside and said to himself, 'I shall never again see my satchel, but at least I have learned a lesson. Never trust a flirting woman.'

Meanwhile, the woman arrived home with the calf and the satchel. As she entered the courtyard, she called, 'Husband, I have returned and I will never leave you again. I have brought the calf and I have brought all the things the thief stole from us.'

There was no answer to her call. So, she tied the calf to a post and ran inside. There she found her husband sweeping the floor. She looked around in amazement. The breakfast was made, the fire was lit, and the washing was hanging on the bushes to dry.

'O stubborn man,' she cried. 'What has happened to you? Why are you not sitting on your bench staring at the sky?'

The husband said, 'I lost my fortune, I lost my face, and I lost my wife because I was so stubborn.'

At once, the wife took the broom and began to sweep. 'Go and sit on your bench,' she said. 'It is for man to order and for woman to obey.'

At that moment, the calf, who had not been fed all day, began to bawl. The husband said, 'I shall water the calf.'

The woman said, 'No, I shall do it.'

The husband said, 'It is for man to order and woman to obey. You shall not water the calf. That is man's work.'

And so he watered the calf that day and every day thereafter, and the husband and wife never quarrelled again.

A. S. Mehdevi

The Robinson affair

Thinking about the story

1 At what point did you realise what Mr Robinson was?
2 What incident makes the family nervous about how Mr Robinson may treat birds?
3 What is the best evidence of how well Mr Robinson behaves towards birds?

Cat's eye view

What do you imagine that Mr Robinson made of the events? Try retelling the story from his point of view. Here are the main events to help you.

- The arrival of the new family

- The attempt to find the cat's owners

- The arrival of Joey, the budgerigar

- Getting near to the cage

- The budgerigar's mimicry

- The new neighbours

Mr Robinson

How would you describe Mr Robinson? This is how students in one class described him.

- 'I think of Mr Robinson as being very secretive and reserved.'

- 'In my view, the cat is just waiting for a chance to get his own back on everyone.'

- 'I think he is one of life's watchers.'

- 'I can imagine him being quite sharp in some of his comments.'

- 'He's just a very easy-going cat.'

- 'I see him as rather formal and very polite.'

- 'I reckon he's the kind of animal who likes to keep everyone thinking.'

What do you think?

Mum takes a bath

Thinking about the poem

What do you think that a diary of one day in this mum's life would look like?
1 Make a list of all the things that are mentioned in the poem.
2 Against each one put a time when you think it might have happened.
3 Now think of other things that might have happened during a 'normal' day in that household.
4 Put times against these too.

Writing

Now write Mum's diary for the day, using all the events you have listed.

Royal mail

Who's who

Stories that are written in the form of letters are always much easier to understand when you have worked out who the characters are and how they are linked.

Copy out this chart and fill in the right-hand column to show how the characters in this story relate to each other.

Character	Comments
Pamela Johnston	
Penelope Johnston	
Jean Sidebotham	
Gertrud Bauscher	
Helga Bauscher	
Muriel Tynte	

Stubborn husband, stubborn wife

Thinking about the story

1 How did you think the story would finish?
2 How do you feel about the way it actually ends: surprised/disappointed/pleased/ annoyed/amused ... or what?
3 Why do you feel like that?
4 Can you imagine a husband and wife being as stubborn as this towards each other nowadays? How might they behave?

Writing

This story is amusing and entertaining, but it also has a serious point. It sets out to teach a lesson. Suppose you wanted to teach a friend of yours the same lesson. Try to think of a modern version of this story that has the same point. Use the same basic ideas, but make all the details suitable for the present day. Now write the story you have thought of. Remember who you are writing for and why you are writing.

Chain letter

The letter Jane received is printed on the next page.

The International Chain Letter

International Schemes Ltd.

Dear Jane

This is the letter you have heard about on TV. You can help break the world record for the longest letter chain ever. All you have to do is send a picture postcard to the first person on the list below and let him or her know a little bit about yourself. Then copy this letter and send it to six of your friends, leaving the first name off the list and adding your own as number six.

If you would like to be kept in touch with how the letter chain is going and to receive a commemorative scroll (with your name on) when the world record is broken, just send a cheque or postal order for £5.00 to: The Official Organiser, International Chain Letter, PO Box 178, Ketchworth, KT4 8LJ. (Please make the cheque payable to 'International Schemes'.) Any profits will be donated to a good cause.

Please write within four days of receiving this letter or the chain will be broken. After 24 days you will receive postcards from all over the world.

This letter started in Rome, Italy, and some very important people have been on the list. Even Buckingham Palace and 10 Downing Street have not broken the chain! You have been sent the letter because you are considered to be reliable. Please do not let all the other participants down.

If you do not break the chain the record will be broken and it will be entered in the Book of Great World Records. Watch out for more news of this attempt on TV and don't forget to send off for your commemorative scroll.

Yours sincerely,

Molly

1. Godfrey Wiltshire, Wood House, Heathcote Road, Classingham, Cambridgeshire
2. Jenny Topleigh, 14 Bushy Road, Penrith, Cumbria, CA27 9RT
3. Tony Bull, 157 Northend Lane, Crystal Palace, London, SE4 2YE
4. Paul Deredawn, Oaktree Lodge, Glassenbury, Gloucestershire, GL5 5PR
5. Elizabeth Drury, 47 Linton Hill, Oxford, OX2 7HU
6. Molly Evans, 39 Courtship Avenue, Bristol, BS18 7OW

Working on your own

1 Read through the letter on page 67 again very carefully.
2 Look at it from Jane's point of view. Write down a list of reasons why she might want to keep the chain letter going.
3 Look at it from Jane's mum's point of view. Write down a list of possible reasons why she might be suspicious of the letter and want to tear it up.

Working with a partner

4 Compare your list with your partner's. Discuss what you have both written. Add any new points to your lists.
5 With your partner, act out the whole conversation between Mum and Jane and carry it on until one of them backs down. (Remember: it's not a row, it's an intelligent discussion.)

Writing

6 Write the conversation between Mum and Jane as a script. For more on setting out a script see page 180.

Group Discussion

Discuss these points in a small group:

1 Have you ever received a chain letter? What did you do?
2 What do you think of chain letters generally?
3 What do you think of the chain letter Jane received?
4 What would you have done if you had received that letter?
5 Do you think Jane's mum should let her decide for herself what to do?

Letters to a newspaper

Mrs Burfoot, Jane's mother, was so angry about the chain letter that she wrote a letter to her local newspaper. She wanted to warn other parents not to let their children become involved. Here is the start of Mrs Burfoot's letter.

A week later the same newspaper printed a letter from Mr Roger Griffin, the Official Organiser of the TV International Chain Letter and Managing Director of International Schemes:

Dear Editor,
My daughter (aged 12) recently received a chain letter which asked her to send a postcard to a total stranger and to send copies of the original letter to six of her friends. My suspicions were aroused by

Dear Editor,
In last week's issue you published a letter from Mrs Susan Burfoot, the mother of a 12 year old girl who had received a copy of the chain letter initiated by my organisation. I would like to reply to Mrs Burfoot's absurd accusations.

In the first place, the whole point of the chain letter is to attempt to break the world record for the longest running chain letter of all time. Any 12 year old would be excited at the opportunity to take part in a record breaking attempt of this kind. I do not see why this mother should feel it is her 'duty' to warn other parents about this bid on the world record. What harm can it do? Surely it can only be a good thing if young people from all parts of the world are in communication with one another, joining each other in a common enterprise.

Secondly, the £5 is to cover the cost of preparing and posting the commemorative scroll. It is clearly stated in the letter that any profit will be donated to charity. Thirdly, it is not stated in the letter that members of the Royal Family or of the Government have given their support to the record attempt. Perhaps your correspondent cannot read.

The International Chain Letter was mentioned on television: on *It's Amazing!* on 5th February, to be precise. Your correspondent does her cause no good when she neglects to check simple matters of fact. As for her point about putting unfair pressure on children, I think her letter makes perfectly plain that the only unfair pressure on her own daughter came from her and not from us. Why can she not allow her daughter to use her own time and pocket money in the way she herself chooses?

Yours sincerely,
Roger Griffin

Writing

Read the letter from Mr Griffin carefully. Work out what Jane's mother must have said in her letter to the newspaper. Write her letter.

Discussion

What do you think of Mr Griffin's letter? Do you think it would persuade Jane's mother that she had nothing to be concerned about?

The invisible beast

The beast that is invisible
is stalking through the park,
but you cannot see it coming
though it isn't very dark.
Oh you know it's out there somewhere
though just why you cannot tell,
but although you cannot see it
it can see you very well.
You sense its frightful features
and its great ungainly form,
and you wish that you were home now
where it's cozy, safe and warm.
And you know it's coming closer
for you smell its awful smell,
and although you cannot see it
it can see you very well.
Oh your heart is beating faster,
beating louder than a drum,
for you hear its footsteps falling
and you body's frozen numb.
And you cannot scream for terror
and your fear you cannot quell,
for although you cannot see it
it can see you very well.

Jack Prelutsky

*T*urn on your radio

The listening public is very apt to jump to conclusions long before it has grasped all the facts. A fine example of this occurred in 1955, when Scandinavian countries were horrified to hear of an earthquake which had shaken Portugal and caused fearful devastation in Lisbon. Had they heard the beginning of the programme, they would have known that, though the information was correct and 30,000 people had been killed, the disaster had occurred two hundred years previously. It was an historical programme which had been up-dated by an opening announcement to the effect that: 'We now interrupt this programme to broadcast an extra news bulletin.'

In some respects, it was similar to a broadcast seventeen years earlier, which had brought panic to parts of North America, and which can reasonably be summed up as the day the Martians invaded the USA.

Strangely enough, the great drama of the men from Mars would probably have never happened, had it not been for a very popular ventriloquist and a considerably less popular singer. The date was Sunday, October 31st, 1938, and the time: 8 pm. By pure coincidence, it was Hallowe'en.

In a studio belonging to the Columbia Broadcasting System in mid-town Manhattan, a party of actors belonging to Orson Welles' 'Mercury Theatre of the Air' was about to broadcast an adaptation of H G Wells' novel *The War of the Worlds*. It was during a period of considerable tension.

One month earlier, the British Prime Minister, Neville Chamberlain, had made a flying visit to Munich. After talks with Hitler, he achieved an agreement which helped to postpone the outbreak of World War II by just short of a year.

Those who had been waiting for the troops to march and the guns to fire and the bombs to explode, felt relieved. The prospect of a new war seemed rather like an invitation to the end of the world. But this poor old planet had been reprieved – at least, for the time being. Nevertheless, there was still a good deal of uneasiness. The public in Europe and North America had become conditioned to expect the worst.

The production which Orson Welles and his players were about to enact was not expected to be up to much. A secretary employed by the unit had dismissed it as 'silly', and a studio technician had called it 'dull'. At some point in rehearsal, they even considered doing something else; but the only possible alternative was *Lorna Doone*, and that, they decided, would be even duller.

As for the majority of American listeners, they preferred to tune their sets to another station, where a ventriloquist named Edgar Bergen and his dummy, an amusing puppet named 'Charlie McCarthy', seemed likely to be much more fun. Bergen was at the height of his fame, and pollsters estimated that about thirty per cent of the listeners switched on to his programme – against only three per cent who wished to hear *The War of the Worlds*.

Five minutes after the latter had started, Edgar Bergen's performance came to an end. A rather mediocre singer, who featured well down in the charts, took over. A good many listeners grunted something about not wanting to hear him, and re-tuned their sets. *The War of the Worlds* was now five minutes old, and they had missed the opening announcement that 'The Columbian Broadcasting System and its affiliated stations present Orson Welles and the Mercury Theatre of the Air in *The War of the Worlds* by H. G. Wells.'

Even those who had heard the beginning were in for surprises, and those who had read the book must have found the beginning no less disconcerting. Wells' story is set in the Home Counties. At first it is thought that a meteorite has come to earth near Woking in Surrey. But then it is seen to be a metal cylinder inhabited by unpleasant creatures looking rather like octopuses. The visitors advance on London and create havoc and death before they are slain – not by guns or by flame-throwers, but by bacteria. Systems which had turned out to be impregnable to weapons are destroyed by a bug which was not identified by the author, but which could have been an ordinary flu germ.

In Orson Welles' adaptation the scene was set at Grovers Mill, New Jersey, with New York City as the Martian's eventual target. H. G. Wells told his tale as a straightforward narrative, describing the events from the point of view of one character. Orson Welles' handling of the story was very different.

After the announcement of the programme, a weather forecast was given, and then listeners were told that dance tunes would be relayed from a New York hotel. Suddenly, the music was interrupted by a quick-fire news flash about the invasion from Mars. The rest of the play was narrated by this technique. It was brilliantly done – so brilliantly that the newscasts were a little too realistic. Police telephone switchboards were suddenly flooded with calls from panic-stricken citizens asking for advice.

A report that the invaders were using poison gas caused twenty families from a block of houses in the New Jersey town of Newark to come running out into the street, wet handkerchiefs over their heads and with towels covering their faces. There were more phone calls to the police, asking such questions as 'Are any gas masks available?' and 'Ought I to close my windows?'

In Riverside Drive, New York, something like one hundred people evacuated their homes in readiness for flight; and, in Providence, Rhode

Island, all the lights were switched off to confuse the invaders. In Pittsburgh, a woman tried to poison herself, preferring this kind of death to destruction by the Martians. In Harlem, 'end of the world' prayer meetings were held; a labourer living somewhere in Massachusetts spent all his savings in an attempt to buy his way to safety; at least one man in San Francisco volunteered for the American armed forces; and, way down south in Birmingham, Alabama, the inhabitants gathered together in churches to pray for deliverance from the fearful creatures with leathery skins and death-dealing tentacles.

But, almost as bad, was the second wave of rumours which this fantastic imposter of a broadcast provoked. There were stories of masses of people who, attempting to make a get-away in their cars, were spinning off the roads and choking the ditches. There were tales of the inhabitants of apartment houses moving their furniture into the streets, and even accounts of solid citizens in the Middle-West fleeing to the hills and hiding in caves. These were all untrue, and were not even features of the play. Popular imagination had gone berserk, and there was no knowing where it all might end.

Halfway through the programme, which only lasted about an hour, there was the announcement that: 'You are listening to the CBS presentation of Orson Welles and the Mercury Theatre of the Air in an original dramatisation of *The War of the Worlds* by H. G. Wells. The performance will continue after a brief intermission.' But it came too late. By this time, many listeners had been dislodged from their radio sets by the tide of panic, and the words were spoken to empty rooms.

Eventually, after countless soothing announcements, the truth got through. America, rather shamefacedly and, in some instances, very angrily, went home. The panic was over. The invaders who never came had departed. All was as well as it could be in a nervous world.

But those citizens of the USA who were hoaxed by this all too vivid broadcast were not alone. When, in the following year, an adaptation of the programme was broadcast in Ecuador under the title of *The Men from Mars*, it caused a similar panic. In spite of rumours to the contrary, the only casualty in the United States incident was one young woman, who fell and broke her arm when running downstairs. In Ecuador, where they are presumably more excitable, a mob of indignant listeners burned down the radio station afterwards, and six members of the cast died in the flames.

Richard Garrett

By gum

Death to the Dentist!
Death to his chair!
Death to his 'this might hurt'!
There! There! There!
Death to his injections!
Death to his nurse!
Death to his amalgam!
Curse! Curse! Curse!
Death to his needle!
Death to his drill!
Death to his 'open wides'!
Kill! Kill! Kill!

Spike Milligan

Sad I ams

I am
the ring
from an empty Cola can
the scrapings
from an unwashed porridge pan
the severed arm
of last year's Action Man.
I am
the envelope
on which the gum is gone
the sellotape
where you can't find the end
the toothless stapler, springless bulldog clip
the dried up liquid paper
that mars instead of mends
the stamped addressed reply
that you forgot
to send.
I am
the battery in which no charge is left
the starter motor which remains inert
the tyre on which the tread is worn
the sparking plug which shows no sign of spark
the carburettor choked by bits of dirt
the chromium trim from which the shine has gone.
I am
a garden
overgrown with weeds
a library book
that no one ever reads
a stray
which no one thinks to feed
the piece of good advice
which no one seems to need.

Trevor Millum

I am the song

I am the song that sings the bird.
I am the leaf that grows the land.
I am the tide that moves the
moon.
I am the stream that halts the
sand.
I am the cloud that drives the
storm.
I am the earth that lights the sun.
I am the fire that strikes the
stone.
I am the clay that shapes the
hand.
I am the word that speaks the
man.

Charles Causley

76

The invisible beast

Thinking points

1 Have you ever been frightened by something that you couldn't see?
2 If so, does this poem describe the feelings that you had?
3 Which parts of the poem best capture the feelings that people have about 'the beast that is invisible'?
4 What is the most frightening aspect of the beast in the poem?

Writing

In a way the poem is like a story: it describes what happens when 'you' come across the beast. It describes the place ('through the park') and the time ('it isn't very dark'). On the other hand it isn't a complete story with full details, a beginning, a middle, and an end. These are left to the reader's imagination.

1 Read the poem again. As you read, try to turn the poem into a series of pictures, sounds, smells, and feelings in your head.
2 Jot down the most vivid pictures that you got as you read the poem.
3 Now think about turning those pictures, sounds, smells, and feelings into a short story. You will need:
- a central character
- a story-teller. (This could be the central character, but might be a friend, or someone who watches from a distance. It could even be the invisible beast.)
- a shape. (Decide how it starts, roughly what happens in the middle, and the kind of thing that might happen in the end.)

Turn on your radio

The gist of the story

Check that you have understood the main points of the story by answering these questions.

1 What is it about?
2 When did it happen?
3 What was the story that the broadcast was based on?
4 What were the main ways in which it was changed?
5 Why did a lot of people miss the beginning of the broadcast?
6 What did they think they had tuned in to?
7 What effect did it have on them?

What do you think?

This story raises a number of important questions about broadcasting. As you think about them, remember that in 1938 TV didn't exist, so listening to the radio was almost as widespread as watching TV is today.

1 Whose fault was it that the broadcast made people panic?
2 What, if anything, did the broadcasters do wrong?
3 Many people in the USA were angry at what had been done. Were they right to be angry?
4 What do you think of the behaviour of the people in Ecuador?
5 Many people today believe that characters they see in 'soaps' like *EastEnders* or *Neighbours* are real people, not just actors playing a part. Such characters are invited to public events as if they are real people and receive presents on their 'birthdays'. Why is this? Is it dangerous?

By gum

Pattern poems

As you can see, this poem is written according to a pattern:

> Death to the —!
> Death to his —!
> — — —!
> Death to his —!
> Death to his —!
> Death to his —!
> — — —!

You could use this pattern to write a similar poem about any other person who, in your opinion spoils your life ... like the men who keep digging up your road, or the person who won't let you ride your bike through the park. Think of someone like that to write a similar poem about. But keep it light-hearted by changing the repeated words to 'Down with ...'

Sad I ams

Writing

Choose one of these 'I ams' poems to write.

1 Your own *Sad I ams* poem, listing the things that in your experience are really sad.

2 Change the word 'sad' for one of these words and then make up a poem to fit the title:

Happy	Angry	Frightened
Tired	Fierce	Timid

I am the song

Sorting it out

Although this poem is very short, it packs a lot in. At first sight many of the lines don't seem to make sense: they seem to be back to front. 'I am the clay that shapes the hand' would seem to make more sense if it read 'I am the hand that shapes the clay.' But then it wouldn't really be worth saying. So what can the poem mean when it says 'I am the clay that shapes the hand?' One answer to this question might be that although you do shape the clay when you make a pot or a model, you can only shape it well, if you understand and accept what clay is like. For example, you won't get far if you try to make a working bicycle out of clay. So, as you work with clay, the clay itself teaches your hand what is possible.

Discuss the lines in this way and see how many different ideas you can think of to interpret each one.

Product launch

Every year thousands of new food products are offered to shoppers.
This is your opportunity to produce one for the food industry.

What people want

You can get an idea of this from what people buy. Here are some
of the changes in shopping habits over the last twenty years.

- more brown bread
- less milk
- more frozen vegetables
- less sugar
- more chicken

- less tea
- more margarine
- fewer cakes
- more ready meals

79

What people need

In recent years there has been increasing concern about food additives such as artifical colourings and artificial preservatives. This has forced food manufacturers to choose more 'natural' alternatives when they are available.

There has also been a steady increase in health and wholefood shops. On the other hand, people are eating more burgers, more pizzas and more convenience foods in general. More potatoes are still used in chips than in any other way.

People should eat...

Less salt

We get through two whole teaspoons of salt per day. That's over 4 kilos (9 pounds) a year and this is known to be one of the major causes for high blood pressure and heart disease.

Less sugar

The average person eats 38 kilos (84 pounds) of sugar each year. Much of the sugar will be in sweets, soft drinks and sweet-tasting foods. It may be called sucrose, dextrose, fructose, glucose or maltose but it's still sugar and it's one major reason why 30 per cent of adults are too fat and why 30 per cent do not have a single tooth of their own.

Less fat

Meat, butter, milk, cheese, chips, chocolate, cakes, pastries and pies all have one thing in common: they contain fat, often quite a lot of it. Most people in Britain need to cut down the amount of fat they eat by as much as a quarter. They would be reducing their waistline and, at the same time, reducing the risk of serious illness.

More fibre

Fibre is the name for the carbohydrates found in the cell walls of plants. It is important for health and it makes you feel full up without making you fat. Some high fibre foods are brown bread, baked beans, apples, baked potatoes, nuts, green vegetables and bananas. The average person could happily eat 50 per cent more fibre and still not be eating too much of it.

1 Decide on the food product you are going to launch.
  Think over what you have discovered about what people buy and what is needed for a good diet.
2 Look at the food products on page 79. Decide how you will package your product: what will the box or packet look like and what will it have printed on it?

3 Prepare the advertisement(s) that will launch your new product. You will need to think about what will make it appealing to other people. What are its selling points?

Telling the world

Once your product is prepared and your initial advertising campaign is ready, you want all the extra publicity you can get.

The way that companies tell newspapers, magazines, radio and television about their new ventures is through a press release. This contains enough information to interest journalists in running a short story or contacting you for further information in order to run a longer feature.

Activity

Prepare a press release for your new product. Try to make it sound as different as possible without making impossible claims. Remember that the correct layout is important for the journalist who may use your story. (See below.)

Not to be published until 01:00 March 23.

Munch-it launch

Glutton Ltd., the well known manufacturer of quality foods, have today launched what they believe will be their most successful

For further information, contact:
Sara Chatham, Press Officer,
Glutton Ltd.,
Overeaten Industrial Park,
Lincoln, LN34 2PQ
Tel: 0522 78998

What is in a press release?

This will vary according to the subject but these points may help.

1 First paragraph: the facts about what is happening
2 Middle paragraphs: further information which, in this case, might include:
   - facts about the product
   - why it is needed in our diet
   - results of any market research
   - comments by people who tried it (this might include a well-known person you have contacted to promote the product)
3 Last paragraph: summary – this might include phrases such as 'We believe this product will be...'
4 Final lines: details of person to contact for further information.

81

Crisis for your product

The product that you have so carefully launched has become involved in the food poisoning scare involving Etrium B. You believe that your product is as safe as you can make it and know that to withdraw it would bankrupt your company and throw dozens of people out of work.

FOOD POISONING SCANDAL

Government silent *by E. B. Jones*

The Ministry of Agriculture was refusing last night to confirm or deny reports that cases of Etrium B food poisoning have become far more widespread than the minister claimed in last week's newspaper announcements.

The Etrium B bacillus which has already been blamed for the deaths of seven elderly residents at an old people's home back in December is now thought to have caused eight to ten times as much illness as was previously thought.

Scientists from the microbiology department of Wessex University contacted the minister after last week's press announcement to point out that she had failed to make any allowance in her figures for new foodstuffs.

Etrium B is believed to survive some of the new food processing techniques more easily than it does in more traditional cooking methods. One of the scientists commented: 'A lot of our fancy new foods are riddled with Etrium B and I am willing to name the products if the minister is too cowardly to do her job.'

Last night the Ministry of Agriculture was unwilling to add to its previous statement about the food poisoning scare but a junior official did say: 'There has been a lot of scaremongering about Etrium B. There always has been food poisoning and there always will be. The current outbreaks are no different from those we have experienced in previous years and the government has no intention of changing its policy.'

Meanwhile the opposition spokesperson on health, attacked the government for its 'complacency' and its 'sheer ignorance'. He said, in a speech to party workers earlier today:

'It is impossible to imagine any other country in the world which would treat such a serious matter in such an off-hand way. How many people have to die before the government takes action?'

1 Make a list of the actions you believe you need to take to safeguard the sales of your product. You could consider these points:
- Improve hygiene at the factory.
- Make further health checks on staff.
- Check each stage of production for possible problems.
- Use publicity: there is no proof that products like yours cause this food poisoning.

2 You are visited by a local food inspector. A few days later a report appears in the local press under the headlines:

Health scare at local factory Etrium B suspected

a) Write the rest of the report.
b) Write a letter to the paper defending your factory.

Alone in the grange

Strange,
Strange,
Is the little old man
Who lives in the Grange.
Old,
Old;
And they say that he keeps
A box full of gold.
Bowed,
Bowed,
Is his thin little back
That once was so proud.
Soft,
Soft,
Are his steps as he climbs
The stairs to the loft.
Black,
Black,
Is the old shuttered house.
Does he sleep on a sack?
They say he does magic,
That he can cast spells,
That he prowls round the garden
Listening for bells;
That he watches for strangers,
Hates every soul,
And peers with his dark eye
Through the keyhole.
I wonder, I wonder,
As I lie in my bed,
Whether he sleeps with his hat on his head?
Is he really magician
With altar of stone,
Or a lonely old gentleman
Left on his own?

Gregory Harrison

To be a gardener's boy

At the age of sixteen, to be a gardener's boy seemed to me a good idea. I had been told about this old chap, Buzz, who took on blokes at 8d. an hour – of course, this was before the War – and it was worth 8d. to learn about gardening as a commercial proposition, or, How to Make Gardening Pay...without too much digging. Buzz used to say: 'If you keep chivvying it about, all the goodness evapormorates.'

I used to trail along behind him, like a dutiful disciple, keeping well out of the way of his walking stick, from which I got many a prod, and which he needed on account of his Sciatica, or was it his Gout? Anyway, for business purposes, it was his War wounds.

His first act when investigating a new garden, would be to use that terrible walking-stick, on any flower that had dared to come out earlier than its fellows. Its head would be knocked off instantly. 'It makes the others look backward.'

When I got there each morning he would instruct me in our stratagems for the day. As for instance: The antirrhinums in Mrs Jones' garden had got to be thinned out, and replanted carefully in seed-boxes. These would be taken round to Mrs Brown later on, and offered to her as a favour, being rare specimens, and having been obtained at great trouble and expense – though they had actually been planted by the foresighted Buzz himself, in great profusion, with this end in view.

There were mushrooms to be picked, the spawn having been previously inserted under the lawns at Mrs Smith's and a charge would be made for clearing away such unsightly blemishes.

Then there was the mowing-machine lark. 'Now, we're going round to Mrs Robinson's. She's got a new lawn coming up that wants cutting. Now she ain't got a mower; but Mrs Green 'as, a good 'un. Go round to Mrs Robinson, and tell her her grass wants cutting. Tell her we'll hire a mower. Go to Mrs Green and tell her her mower wants sharpening. Take it round to Mrs Robinson's and mow the lawn. Then, bring it to my place, and we'll leave it there for a couple of days. We'll charge Mrs Green for sharpening the mower: 7/6. Charge Mrs Robinson for hire of the mower: 7/6. And the labour: five bob.'

'But Mr Buzz, that mower doesn't want sharpening. I sharpened it myself, don't you remember – last week?'

'Grow up. Grow up. Of course it doesn't need sharpening. Don't cher know nothing? Ain'tcher never 'eard on Business?'

We had great crops of tomatoes growing in everybody's garden; all out of sight, at the back of the compost-heap. In the very largest garden, Buzz grew his marrers. Buzz hadn't got a garden of his own – he didn't need one.

Sometimes a bit of luck would come our way. Somebody would want to get rid of their rockery; demolishing rockeries is heavy work – and expensive. But you could be sure that before the first barrow-load had been wheeled away, somebody living nearby would have been persuaded that a rockery was just what they needed, complete with rare, expensive plants, all at bargain prices.

I had been with Buzz for about a year, when I got a better job. The last thing I remember about him was true to form, though this time he didn't mean to do it.

I told him I had been left £5 by an uncle.

'Cor. Just what I need. You can do yourself a bit of good 'ere. Now I got a really big job on, and I need £5 to buy the plants and seeds. I'll pay you back double.'

Like a mug, I lent him the five quid. What did he do? He went and pegged out. And that was that.

Edward Sebley

The man of the family

The man of the family, who swears at his widowed mother
And smokes in the house. She appeals to the Staff for help
On Parents' Evening, in tears, for the character-training
Of caning, lines and keeping-in after school,
And in his cowardly way he comes to heel;
But falls deadweight on her or anyone
Soft enough not to stand up to him,
Opening locker doors in smaller boys' faces
And shutting desklids on their heads and fingers.

Stanley Cook

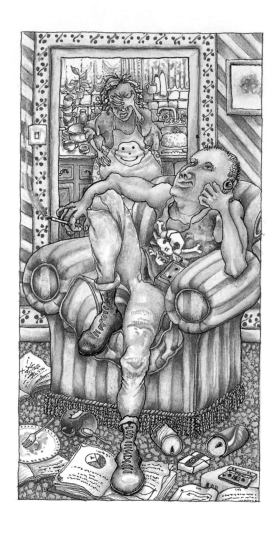

School champion

Learn he could not; he said he could not learn;
But he professed it gave him no concern:
Books were his horror, dinner his delight,
And his amusement to shake hands and fight;
Argue he could not, but in case of doubt,
Or disputation, fairly boxed it out:
This was his logic, and his arm so strong,
His cause prevailed, and he was never wrong.

George Crabbe

Charles

The day Laurie started kindergarten he renounced corduroy overalls with bibs and began wearing blue jeans with a belt; I watched him go off the first morning with the older girl next door, seeing clearly that an era of my life was ended, my sweet-voiced nursery-school tot replaced by a long-trousered, swaggering character who forgot to stop at the corner and wave goodbye to me.

He came home the same way, the front door slamming open, his cap on the floor, and the voice suddenly became raucous shouting, 'Isn't anybody here?'

At lunch he spoke insolently to his father, spilled Jannie's milk, and remarked that his teacher said that we were not to take the name of the Lord in vain.

'How was school today?' I asked, elaborately casual.

'All right,' he said.

'Did you learn anything?' his father asked.

Laurie regarded his father coldly. 'I didn't learn nothing,' he said.

'Anything,' I said. 'Didn't learn anything.'

'The teacher spanked a boy, though,' Laurie said, addressing his bread and butter. 'For being fresh,' he added with his mouth full.

'What did he do?' I asked. 'Who was it?'

Laurie thought. 'It was Charles,' he said. 'He was fresh. The teacher spanked him and made him stand in a corner. He was awfully fresh.'

'What did he do?' I asked again, but Laurie slid off his chair, took a cookie, and left, while his father was still saying, 'See here, young man.'

The next day Laurie remarked at lunch, as soon as he sat down, 'Well, Charles was bad again today.' He grinned enormously and said, 'Today Charles hit the teacher.'

'Good heavens,' I said, mindful of the Lord's name, 'I suppose he got spanked again?'

'He sure did,' Laurie said. 'Look up,' he said to his father.

'What?' his father said, looking up.

'Look down,' Laurie said. 'Look at my thumb. Gee, you're dumb.' He began to laugh insanely.

'Why did Charles hit the teacher?' I asked quickly.

'Because she tried to make him colour with red crayons,' Laurie said. 'Charles wanted to colour with green crayons so he hit the teacher and she spanked him and said nobody play with Charles but everybody did.'

The third day – it was Wednesday of the first week – Charles bounced a see-saw onto the head of a little girl and made her bleed and the teacher made him stay inside all during recess. Thursday Charles had to stand in a corner during story-time because he kept pounding his feet on the floor. Friday Charles was deprived of blackboard privileges because he threw chalk.

On Saturday I remarked to my husband, 'Do you think kindergarten is too unsettling for Laurie? All this toughness and bad grammar, and this Charles boy sounds like such a bad influence.'

'It'll be all right,' my husband said reassuringly. 'Bound to be people like Charles in the world. Might as well meet them now as later.'

On Monday Laurie came home late, full of news. 'Charles,' he shouted as he came up the hill; I was waiting anxiously on the front steps, 'Charles,' Laurie yelled all the way up the hill, 'Charles was bad again.'

'Come right in,' I said, as soon as he came close enough. 'Lunch is waiting.'

'You know what Charles did?' he demanded, following me through the door. 'Charles yelled so in school they sent a boy in from first grade to tell the teacher she had to make Charles keep quiet, and so Charles had to stay after school. And so all the children stayed to watch him.'

'What did he do?' I asked.

'He just sat there,' Laurie said, climbing into his chair at the table. 'Hi Pop, y'old dust mop.'

'Charles had to stay after school today,' I told my husband.

'Everyone stayed with him.'

'What does this Charles look like?' my husband asked Laurie. 'What's his other name?'

'He's bigger than me,' Laurie said. 'And he doesn't have any rubbers and he doesn't ever wear a jacket.'

Monday night was the first Parent-Teachers meeting, and only the fact that Jannie had a cold kept me from going; I wanted passionately to meet Charles's mother. On Tuesday Laurie remarked suddenly, 'Our teacher had a friend come see her in school today,'

'Charles's mother?' my husband and I asked simultaneously.

'Naaah,' Laurie said scornfully. 'It was a man who came and made us do exercises. Look.' He climbed down from his chair and squatted down and touched his toes. 'Like this,' he said. He got solemnly back into his chair and said, picking up his fork, 'Charles didn't even do exercises.'

'Fresh again?' I said.

'He kicked the teacher's friend,' Laurie said. 'The teacher's friend told Charles to touch his toes like I just did and Charles kicked him.'

'What are they going to do about Charles, do you suppose?' Laurie's father asked him.

Laurie shrugged elaborately. 'Throw him out of the school, I guess,' he said.

Wednesday and Thursday were routine; Charles yelled during story hour and hit a boy in the stomach and made him cry. On Friday Charles stayed after school again and so did all the other children.

With the third week of kindergarten Charles was an institution in our family; Jannie was being a Charles when she cried all afternoon; Laurie did a Charles when he filled his wagon full of mud and pulled it through the kitchen; even my husband, when he caught his elbow in the telephone cord and pulled telephone, ash tray, and a bowl of flowers off the table, said, after the first minute, 'Looks like Charles.'

During the third and fourth weeks there seemed to be a reformation in Charles; Laurie reported grimly at lunch on Thursday of the third week, 'Charles was so good today the teacher gave him an apple.'

'What?' I said, and my husband added warily, 'You mean Charles?'

'Charles.' Laurie said. 'He gave the crayons around and he picked up the books afterward and the teacher said he was her helper.'

'What happened?' I asked incredulously.

'He was her helper, that's all,' Laurie said, and shrugged.

'Can this be true, about Charles?' I asked my husband that night. 'Can something like this happen?'

'Wait and see,' my husband said cynically. 'When you've got a Charles to deal with, this may mean he's only plotting.'

He seemed to be wrong. For over a week Charles was the teacher's helper; each day he handed things out and he picked things up; no one had to stay after school.

'The PTA meeting's next week again,' I told my husband one evening. 'I'm going to find Charles's mother there.'

'Ask her what happened to Charles,' my husband said. 'I'd like to know.'

'I'd like to know myself,' I said.

On Friday of that week things were back to normal.

'You know what Charles did today?' Laurie demanded at the lunch table, in a voice slightly awed. 'He told a little girl to say a word and she said it and the teacher washed her mouth out with soap and Charles laughed.'

'What word?' his father asked unwisely, and Laurie said, 'I'll have to whisper it to you, it's so bad.' He got down off his chair and went around to his father. His father bent his head down and Laurie whispered joyfully. His father's eyes widened.

'Did Charles tell the little girl to say that?' he asked respectfully.

'She said it twice,' Laurie said. 'Charles told her to say it twice.'

'What happened to Charles?' my husband asked.

'Nothing,' Laurie said. 'He was passing out the crayons.'

Monday morning Charles abandoned the little girl and said the evil word himself three or four times, getting his mouth washed out with soap each time. He also threw chalk.

My husband came to the door with me that evening as I set out for the PTA meeting. 'Invite her over for a cup of tea after the meeting,' he said. 'I want to get a look at her.'

'If only she's there,' I said prayerfully.

'She'll be there,' my husband said. 'I don't see how they could hold a PTA meeting without Charles's mother.'

At the meeting I sat restlessly, scanning each comfortable matronly face, trying to determine which one hid the secret of Charles. None of them looked to me haggard enough. No one stood up in the meeting and apologised for the way her son had been acting. No one mentioned Charles.

After the meeting I identified and sought out Laurie's kindergarten teacher. She had a plate with a cup of tea and a piece of chocolate cake; I had a plate with a cup of tea and a piece of marshmallow cake. We manoeuvred up to one another cautiously and smiled.

'I've been so anxious to meet you,' I said. 'I'm Laurie's mother.'

'We're all so interested in Laurie,' she said.

'Well, he certainly likes kindergarten,' I said. 'He talks about it all the time.'

'We had a little trouble adjusting, the first week or so,' she said primly, ' but now he's a fine little helper. With lapses, of course.'

'Laurie usually adjusts very quickly,' I said. 'I suppose this time it's Charles's influence.'

'Charles?'

'Yes,' I said, laughing, 'you must have your hands full in that kindergarten, with Charles.'

'Charles?' she said. 'We don't have any Charles in the kindergarten.'

Shirley Jackson

Useful person

We'd missed the train. Two hours to wait
On Lime Street Station, Liverpool,
With not a single thing to do.
The bar was shut and Dad was blue
And Mum was getting in a state
And everybody felt a fool.
Yes, we were very glum indeed,
Myself, I'd nothing new to read,
No sweets to eat, no game to play.
'I'm bored,' I said, and straight away,
Mum said what I knew she'd say:
'Go on, then, read a book, OK?'
'I've read them both!' 'That's no excuse.'
Dad sat sighing, 'What a day...
This is precious little use.
I wish they'd open up that bar.'
They didn't, though. No way.
And everybody else was sitting
In that waiting-room and knitting,
Staring, scratching, yawning, smoking.
'All right, Dad?' 'You must be joking!
This is precious little use.
It's like a prison. Turn me loose!'
('Big fool, act your age!' Mum hisses.
'Sorry, missus.'
'Worse than him, you are,' said Mum.)
It was grim. It was glum.

And then the Mongol child came up,
Funny-faced:
Something in her body wrong,
Something in her mind
Misplaced:
Something in her eyes was strange:
What, or why, I couldn't tell:
But somehow she was beautiful
As well.
Anyway, she took us over!
'Hello, love,' said Dad. She said,
'There, sit there!' and punched a spot
On the seat. The spot was what,
Almost, Mum was sitting on,
So Dad squeezed up, and head-to-head,
And crushed-up, hip-to-hip, they sat.

92

'What next, then?' 'Kiss!' 'Oh no, not that!'
Dad said, chuckling. 'Kiss!'
They did!
I thought my Mum would flip her lid
With laughing. Then the Mongol child
Was filled with pleasure – she went wild,
Running round the tables, telling
Everyone to kiss and yelling
Out to everyone to sit
Where she said. They did, too. It
Was sudden happiness because
The Mongol child
Was what she was:
Bossy, happy, full of fun,
And just determined everyone
Should have a good time too! We knew
That's what we'd got to do.
Goodness me, she took us over!
All the passengers for Dover,
Wolverhampton, London, Crewe –
Everyone from everywhere
Began to share
Her point of view! The more they squeezed,
And laughed, and fooled about, the more
The Mongol child
Was pleased!

Dad had to kiss another Dad
('Watch it, lad!' 'You watch it, lad!'
'Stop: you're not my kind of bloke!')
Laugh? I thought that Mum would choke!
And so the time whirled by. The train
Whizzed us home again
And on the way I thought of her:
Precious little use is what
Things had been. Then she came
And things were not
The same!
She was precious, she was little,
She was useful too:
Made us speak when we were dumb,
Made us smile when we were blue,
Cheered us up when we were glum,
Lifted us when we were flat:
Who could be
More use than that?
Mongol child,
Funny-faced,
Something in your body wrong,
Something in your mind
Misplaced,
Something in your eyes, strange:
What, or why, I cannot tell:
I thought you were beautiful:
Useful, as well.

Kit Wright

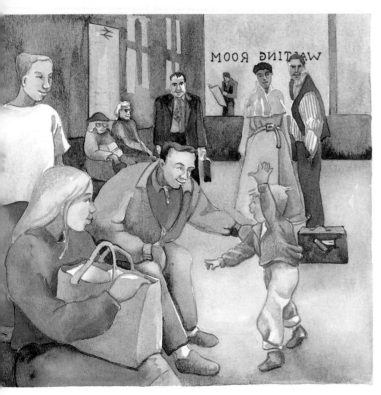

Noh lickle twang!

(Not even a little accent)

Me glad fe se's you come back bwoy,
But lawd yuh let me dung,
Me shame o' yuh soh till all o'
Me proudness drop a grung.
Yuh mean yuh goh dah 'Merica
An spen six whole mont' deh,
An come back not a piece betta
Dan how yuh did goh wey?
Bwoy yuh noh shame? Is soh you come?
Afta yuh tan soh lang!
Not even lickle language bwoy?
Not even little twang?
An yuh sista wat work ongle
One week wid 'Merican
She talk so nice now dat we have
De jooce fe undastan?
Bwoy yuh couldn' improve yuhself!
An yuh get soh much pay?
Yuh spen six mont' a foreign, and
Come back ugly same way?
Not even a drapes trouziz? or
A pass de rydim coat?
Bwoy not even a gole teet or
A gole chain roun yuh t'roat.
Suppose me las' me pass go introjooce
Yuh to a stranga
As me lamented son wat lately
Come from 'Merica!
Dem hooda laugh afta me, bwoy
Me could'n tell dem soh!
Dem hooda sey me lie, yuh was
A-spen time back a Mocho.
Noh back-ansa me bwoy, yuh talk
Too bad; shet up yuh mout,
Ah doan know how yuh and yuh puppa
Gwine to meck it out.
Ef yuh want please him meck him tink
Yuh bring back someting new.
Yuh always call him 'Pa', dis evenin'
Wen him come sey 'Poo'.

Louise Bennett

Alone in the grange

Writing

1 Think about similar stories which have grown up (or could have grown up) around people known to you. Tell one of them.

2 You might have seen an incident take place and wondered what events led up to it; you might have seen a person and wondered what sort of life he/she had had. Describe, briefly, who or what you actually saw, and what thoughts quickly went through your mind.

3 Write down a selection of at least ten adjectives. They can be twenty words which you pick from this book, or you can think of them yourself. They do not have to be connected in any way. Now look at the first twenty lines of the poem. You will see the pattern that those lines follow. They are based on five adjectives. From your list of twenty, pick any five you like and write a twenty-line poem in the pattern of *Alone in the Grange*.

4 Imagine the sort of life that the 'little old man' in the poem has led. Write his story.

To be a gardener's boy

1 What seems odd about the '8d (about 3p) an hour' which is mentioned in the second sentence?

2 In your own words, what was Buzz's opinion of digging?

3 'Anyway, for business purposes, it was his war wounds.' Why was this, do you think?

4 What are 'stratagems'?

5 Why did Buzz not have a garden of his own?

6 What were Buzz's four money-making schemes mentioned here? Explain one of them in your own words.

7 Why did the author not get back the £5 which he lent to Buzz? Which phrase tells us? how many more phrases do you know which mean the same thing?

8 In this passage, 'How to make Gardening Pay' is one of Buzz's sayings. It is given capital letters. Are there any other words which you are surprised to find given capital letters? Why have capital letters been used, do you think?

School champion/The man of the family

Bully, hooligan, thug , strong man, trouble-maker

1 Which of these titles do you think is most appropriate for each poem?

2 Why?

3 How would you describe each boy?

4 Which boy's behaviour do you think is worse and why?

5 Think about the titles of the poems. What do you think is the purpose behind each of the titles?

Charles

Thinking about the story

1 What impression do you get of Laurie from the way he behaves at home?
2 What do you think of the way his parents treat him at home?
3 Why do you think Laurie makes up the character of Charles?
4 Did you guess the truth about 'Charles' before the end of the story? If you did, what led you to? If not, how did you feel when you realised?
5 What parts of the story did you find to be most true to life?
6 What parts of the story did you find to be least true to life?

Writing

1 If Laurie's school had chosen to keep an incident file on his behaviour what do you imagine might be in it? Copy and complete this page from the Incident File.

> **Incident File**
> **Name:** Laurie Jackson
> **Report:**

2 Write a short scene that might occur between Laurie's parents when his mum returns from the PTA meeting. If you are uncertain about using play form, you can check details on page 180.

Useful person

Group reading

1 Read it through on your own and think about how it should be read.
2 Discuss how to divide it up to make an interesting group reading.
3 Decide who should read each part.
4 Practise your group reading.

Thinking points

People sometimes find it difficult to know how they should behave with people who are handicapped (like Downs Syndrome children, or 'Mongols' as they used to be called.)
1 Why do you think this is?
2 What might have happened in the waiting room when the 'Mongol child' came in?
3 Why did she change things?
4 Kit Wright describes her as 'beautiful' and also as 'useful'. Why do you think he chose those two adjectives?
5 What were your thoughts and feelings after reading the poem?

Noh lickle twang

Writing

Yuh mean yuh goh dah 'Merica
An spen six whole mont' deh,
An come back not a piece betta
Dan how yuh did goh wey?

Make up a similar conversation set in a place that you know well. A young person has just spent six months in America, or somewhere else 'exotic' and has returned to meet an older member of the family, or a friend, who expects them to have changed a lot since the two of them last met. The older person is very critical that they haven't changed. Write the conversation (and if possible, write in a dialect that is familiar to you.)

Dialect

Take a short section of the poem (4 or 5 lines) and write two different versions of what it says:
1 In Standard English;
2 In another dialect.

Gulliver

Shipwreck

4th May 1699

Today I set sail from Bristol, aboard the Antelope, as ship's Surgeon.

2nd November 1699

The storm has now blown itself out. We find ourselves somewhere north of Van Diemens Land. Twelve of the crew have died since we left England – Some from exhaustion and some from lack of proper food. There are scarcely enough left to man the ship.

5th November 1699

The Captain has told us that another storm, more violent than the last will strike the ship soon.

After all his adventures, Gulliver has his story published. You are Gulliver and you are going to tell the story of what happened.

1. Read the diary extracts. They miss out quite a lot of his adventures. You will have to use your imagination to fill in some of the gaps.
2. Describe the main things that happened between 4th May and 5th November 1699.
3. Look at the pictures. Work out what happened to Gulliver. Think about what he must have been feeling while all this was happening.
4. Tell the story of what happened to him from the moment when the storm struck.

What to do

This is what happened to Gulliver when he woke up on the morning after the shipwreck. He found himself the prisoner of the people of Lilliput (the Lilliputians).

1   Study the pictures carefully and work out exactly what is going on.
2   Think about all this from Gulliver's point of view. What could he see and hear at each stage? How soon could he work out what was happening? What were his thoughts? What were his feelings?
3   Now tell the story, as if you were Gulliver.

Body search

For a while, Gulliver remained a prisoner.
As part of the bargain he made to get his freedom,
he agreed to let the Lilliputians search his pockets.
This is what happened...

I took the two officers in my hands, put them first into my coat-pockets, and then into every other pocket about me. These gentlemen made an exact inventory of everything they saw.

In the right coat pocket of the Great Man Mountain, after the strictest search we found only one great piece of coarse cloth, large enough to be a foot-cloth for your Majesty's chief room of State. In the left pocket we saw a huge silver chest, with a cover of the same metal, which we were not able to lift. We desired it should be opened.

What to do

1 Read the extracts from the officers' inventory and study the illustration. Now list the objects they discovered in Gulliver's pockets.

2 The officers had to give their king a list and descriptions of everything they found. You can see from the extracts how difficult it was for them to understand these things.
Write descriptions of the other objects they discovered which are pictured above.

3 Add to the list two more things that they might have found in Gulliver's pockets, describing them in the same way.

Out of the right fob pocket hung a great silver chain with a wonderful kind of engine at the bottom. We directed him to draw out whatever was fastened to that chain, which appeared to be a globe, half of silver, and half of some transparent metal; for on the transparent side we saw certain strange figures circularly drawn, and thought we could touch them till we found our fingers stopped by the lucid substance. He put this engine to our ears, whcih made an incessant noise like that of a watermill; and we conjecture it is either some unknown animal, or the god that he worships; but we are more inclined to the latter opinions because he assured us that he seldom did anything without consulting it.

War is avoided

Not far from the Island of Lilliput is another island, Blefuscu. The two countries have been enemies for many years, but now it seems that the people of Blefuscu are planning to invade Lilliput. Gulliver agrees to try to find a way to help stop this invasion.

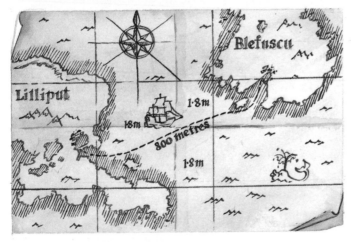

What to do

These pictures show part of what happened, when Gulliver set out to stop the invasion of Lilliput by the people of Blefuscu.

1 Work out what else must have happened.
2 Tell Gulliver's version of the story.

Other adventures of Gulliver

Gulliver eventually escaped from Lilliput. In the course of his life as a traveller and sailor he had many other adventures and met many strange creatures, in many strange lands.

Brobdingnag

Laputa

The land of the Houyhnhms

What to do

1 Choose one of the pictures to work on.
2 Decide what life must have been like for Gulliver in this strange land.
3 Think about how he came to be there.
4 Think about what adventures he might have had while he was there.
5 Think about how he might have escaped.
6 Tell the story of what happened.

Killer whale

I saw it from the back yard first thing in the morning swimming between May Island and the shore – a black boomerang that ripped open the firth, shot up higher than the lighthouse, crossing the white orbits of the gannets, and crashed back into the sea with mountains of snow cascading to the clouds.

I ran up the stairs to George's house.

He was standing at his open window, already fully dressed, and the pages of his bible fluttering in the blue breeze from the sea. His spyglass was at his eye.

'What is it, Gramps? Can I see?

He handed me the glass, and I looked, and saw for the first time, close, the savage cut and thrust of that living scimitar slashing and thrashing the waves, the battling bull head, the powerful fin, and the tigerish tail that mauled the water, churning it like a propellor.

'What is it?' I shouted. 'Is it a whale?'

'Aye, they call it a whale,' George said, 'but it's liker a wolf.'

'Is it like the ones you used to hunt for?' I asked.

'No,' he said quietly, 'that's a killer out there. And compared to the beasts I went after, that one is a butcher, let me tell you, a bad black butcher.'

He told me how he had seen a pack of killers tear out the tongue of one of the great blue whales.

'It was nearly ninety feet long,' he said, 'and its tongue in its jaws must have weighed a ton. They just ripped it out and fed on it while it was bleeding to death from the mouth.'

'Didn't you catch killer whales, Gramps?'

He turned, and I saw his back making for the door.

'Come with me,' he said.

I followed him down to the lumber room of the old house. It was like the interior of a shipwreck – everywhere there were broken bits of everything that had to do with the fishing. He clambered stiffly over the piles of torn nets, long since mouse-eaten, dog-torn and condemned, throwing aside shredded baskets and boxes and punctured dahns in his struggle to reach what he was after. I frisked after him on all fours, sniffing at this and that. He was in the corner, tugging heavily at a stiff tarpaulin draped on a long pole.

'Pull it off,' he breathed, 'you that has so much life in you.'

He tilted the pole and I pulled at the faded green sheeting which came away – and my mouth opened wide.

It was his old harpoon.

Nine feet of lacquered larch and a further foot of solid iron, tipped with the most brutal barb that made even a gartlin hook seem like a bent pin. The everyday working weapon of my great grandfather's youth, unveiled after half a century – now standing upright and shining in the bright windowed corner of a local museum.

'Can you handle it?' he asked.

He did not wait to see.

I followed him through the transe and into the yard, amazed at the sheer weight and size of the arrow that hurt the whale to the heart. We looked out at the killer, still wounding the firth like a vicious vandalising ploughshare.

'That fish wasn't made by God,' the old man said, buttoning his jacket as the wind came up stronger with the brightening sun. 'Do you know what it will do? It will slash open the bellies of seals for sheer sport and leave them dying among the rocks. It will bite the heads off their bairns just out of its badness.'

He steadied himself against the galluses and reached out for his old weapon.

'I'll tell you this, too. If I had seventy years off my back I'd take that harpoon and a boat, and I'd go out there right now and bring about the death of that brute in the name of the Lord.'

I looked at him as he stood beside me white and trembly, putting up his hand to his blurred old eye.

'But this is the nearest I'll ever come now to a whale.'

The first surge of sorrow for one of my own family. One whom I should never have dared dream of pitying. But just a few short years of my life had begun in him the slow stiffening which was a rehearsal for his death.

I looked away from him and out again at the whale, still whipping the waves into a welter of white foam.

'I think it's coming in, Gramps!'

He peered hard over the rooftops.

'So it is,' he said slowly. 'It's coming in to shore. It's coming in to die.'

The killer came in with the forenoon tide and the ebb left it stranded in the harbour by the late afternoon, stuck in the mud between the middle and the east pier. Everyone that was alive and walking that day came down to stare at it... Strung out along piers and street, the galleries of folk scrutinised its immobility, its utter possession of agony. The old men said that it was being slowly crushed by its terrific weight, the vanquished victor victim now to its own bullying bulk; the pitiless unpitied.

When they saw its helplessness the swaggering boys began to descend the steps, plodding soggily across the mud to within a few feet of it. The whale ignored them. Trapped inside its carcass, and netted in air, it could do nothing. Only its tail flapped idly like a tangle at low tide. Closer they came, the brave ones, till they could reach out and touch the torpedo itself in its defused, defenceless state. They landed puny punches on the very tip of the slumped warhead, jumping backwards with cracking halloos as though expecting an explosion. Undetonated, it seemed as invulnerable as the air around it, and their vain grimacings as grotesque as their blows.

Then the first of the boldest clambered onto the big back, near to the tail end, clutching at the hulk with his hand and feet as if he were hanging on to the edge of the Himalayas by a hinge of hair. The whale gave no reaction and the boy was joined by two others. They stood like victorious climbers on their cheap-won summit, arms aloft, cheering. The crowd did no cheering at first, but someone threw them down a flag to stick in its back. Mad matadors mocking the bull. So some people started to laugh.

This was what gave me the sudden glorious idea of bringing down George's harpoon. I ran home fast and stood outside the house taking slow deep breaths before creeping in soft-footed to the lumber room where the mighty arrow was back in its green quiver. But George's hearing was not what it was. His ears were filled with fog. I hurried back to the harbour, frightened in case everyone had gone.

They were in full attendance. The game had reached another stage, and the whale was now crawling with boys, who were taking it in turns to drop pennies down the blow-hole. Seconds after being dropped in, the pennies were shot high into the sky, to the roars of the crowd and much hand-clapping. Many of them were now openly appreciating the sport, to the extent of taking small bets on heads or tails. And each time it sent the coin spinning into the air, the stung whale smashed its tail madly into the mud, sending a boy or two slithering to a soft but dirty landing.

Then people started to notice my harpoon, and a small circle of grinning faces formed itself for me in the crowd. I brandished it clumsily, shouting to the boys down below to watch out for it.

One man climbed onto a pile of fish-boxes.

'Thar she blo-oo-ows!'

He flung back his head and pointed.

Great was my encouragement.

'Gangway, there, out the road, you folks! The boy here is going to let him have it, aren't you? Right between the eyes.'

The size of the stage, the audience, and the real life prop which I found myself holding, suddenly made me into a pygmy.

'No,' I said, sullen and blushing, 'My Gramps will do it.'

They all laughed hugely.

'What, old Geordie Marr? He couldn't throw a fit these days! Let's see how you can throw.'

The picture of an enraged silver lion flashed behind my eyebrows, gripping in his bearded jaws a wolf in sheep's clothing, heaving him down the steps and out of the fold. I saw my great grandfather's withered white arm, seventy years of sap taken out of it, bend suddenly like a sapling to the renewed gale of his youth and fury. My own arm knew then what it was to be his. It uncoiled, and the harpoon spun whistling like a javelin from the pier, travelled through space for a terrible eternity of sixty feet. It sang in the skull of the whale for a brutal bone-crushing second, ending its misery, swayed there like a pine tree in the wind, creaking in the held breath of the crowd.

The crowd released its voice then, and I opened my eyes and saw the harpoon sticking stupidly in the mud. I had achieved a throw of maybe five feet.

Hoots and jeers all round. The whale lay like a black Christ. Loathing opened in me like a wound, the seepage from the stigma.

A coarse drunkard called Bert Mackie leapt onto the whale and shouted to the people that he would now spend a different kind of penny in the blowhole.

'We'll see if it survives my harpoon!' he brayed boozily.

The women shrieked, demented, and the air cracked with the whinnyings of the old men.

That was when the minister arrived.

In a kirk silence he materialised in the mud and told Bert to come down. Instead Bert began to execute a vulgar parody of the hornpipe on the whale's back.

The Reverend Kinnear heaved himself up. Without wasting another word he drove his fist straight into the slack side of the drunkard's leering jaw. Bert teetered on one leg for a fraction, then he crashed crazily into the sucking slime, where he lay like a log.

The minister was still standing on the humped whale, quieter now without its tormentors. Everybody waited to hear what he would say. He was breathing fiercely through flared nostrils, his eyes like live coals. His huge fingers were clenching and unclenching, white and red.

But he could not speak for rage. He jumped down and sank up to his ankles. Nobody laughed. Then he strode with soiled shoes and red face across the harbour bed.

'Get me a hose!' he roared as he came up the steps.

A long hose pipe was produced within seconds.

He attached it himself to the tap outside Harry's office, drew it along Shore Street, and pointed it over the wall at the silent whale.

'Turn it on!'

A fountain of fresh water flowered brightly in the sky and fell. The whale was engulfed in a well of life. A great sigh rippled through its whole slow length and everybody seemed to sigh along with it, seeing its last need fulfilled.

But the Reverend Kinnear stayed there himself all through the rest of the afternoon and into evening, hosing down the grateful killer until the first fingers of blue tide touched its dying sides. He made two men with

motor yawls tie ropes to its tail, and he went along with them, towing it slowly out of the harbour and releasing it a mile off shore.

And there it died.

But for weeks after that it was washed up at different places along the coast, haunting one harbour after another on the flood tides. Finally it came to rest on the west rocks, just where the Old Kirk spread its grave-green skirts down to the sea. By this time it was stinking.

Kinnear preached a sermon about it.

'O, thy offence is rank, it smells to heaven!' he told his congregation.

One that was helpless had come to them lacking water – and they gave it gall. The dog returneth to his vomit, and wickedness winds its way back to the nostril of the sinner, the owner of that foul disease, indifference; hardness; lack of charity.

When George heard what Kinnear had preached he grunted and grumbled.

'He should go to the whales,' he said. 'He'd not come back with a bleeding heart for killers.'

'You could have harpooned it, Gramps,' I said, siding with him, and remembering my own sorry throw. 'You could have killed it when it was stuck in the mud.'

I looked at his quiet arms.

'No, I couldn't,' he said. 'It wouldn't have been fair that way. But if it had been seventy years ago it could have taken its chances with me in the sea, and I'd have brained it stone dead.'

Christopher Rush
from *A Twelvemonth and a Day*

108

The old sea-dog

My father kept the 'Admiral Benbow' inn, and a brown old seaman, with a sabre cut, took up his lodging under our roof.

I remember him as if it were yesterday, as he came plodding to the inn door, his sea-chest following behind him in a hand-barrow; a tall, strong, heavy, nut-brown man; his tarry pigtail falling over the shoulders of his soiled blue coat; his hands ragged and scarred, with black, broken nails; and the sabre cut across one cheek, a dirty, livid white. I remember him looking round the cove and whistling to himself as he did so, and then breaking out in that old sea-song that he sang so often afterwards:

'Fifteen men on The Dead Man's Chest –
Yo-ho-ho, and a bottle of rum!'

in the high, old tottering voice that seemed to have been tuned and broken at the capstan bars. Then he rapped on the door with a bit of stick like a handspike that he carried, and when my father appeared, called roughly for a glass of rum. This, when it was brought to him, he drank slowly, like a connoisseur, lingering on the taste, and still looking about him at the cliffs and up at our signboard.

'This is a handy cove,' says he, at length; 'and a pleasant sittyated grog-shop. Much company, mate?'

My father told him no, very little company, the more was the pity.

'Well, then,' said he, 'this is the berth for me. Here you, matey,' he cried to the man who trundled the barrow; 'bring up alongside and help up my chest. I'll stay here a bit,' he continued. 'I'm a plain man; rum and bacon and eggs is what I want, and that head up there for to watch ships off. What you mought call me? You mought call me captain. Oh, I see what you're at – there'; and he threw down three or four gold pieces on the threshold. 'You can tell me when I've worked through that,' says he, looking as fierce as a commander.

And, indeed, bad as his clothes were, and coarsely as he spoke, he had none of the appearance of a man who sailed before the mast; but seemed like a mate or skipper, accustomed to be obeyed or to strike. The man who came with the barrow told us the mail had set him down the morning before at the 'Royal George'; that he had inquired what inns there were along the coast, and hearing ours well spoken of, I suppose, and described as lonely, had chosen it from the others for his place of residence. And that was all we could learn of our guest.

He was a very silent man by custom. All day he hung round the cove, or upon the cliffs, with a brass telescope; all evening he sat in a corner of the parlour next the fire, and drank rum and water very strong. Mostly he would not speak when spoken to; only look up sudden and fierce, and blow through his nose like a fog-horn; and we and the people who came about our house soon learned to let him be. Every day, when he came back from his stroll, he would ask if any seafaring men had gone by along the road. At first we thought it was the want of company of his own kind that made him ask this question; but at last we began to see he was desirous to avoid them. When a seaman put up at the 'Admiral Benbow' (as now and then some did, making by the coast road for Bristol), he would look in at him through the curtained door before he entered the parlour; and he was always sure to be as silent as a mouse when any such was present. For me, at least, there was no secret about the matter; for I was, in a way, a sharer in his alarms. He had taken me aside one day, and promised me a silver fourpenny on the first of every month if I would only keep my 'weather-eye open for a seafaring man with one leg', and let him know the moment he appeared. Often enough, when the first of the month came round, and I applied to him for my wage, he would only blow through his nose at me, and stare me down; but before the week was out he was sure to think better of it, bring me my fourpenny piece, and repeat his orders to look out for 'the seafaring man with one leg'.

How that personage haunted my dreams, I need scarcely tell you. On stormy nights, when the wind shook the four corners of the house, and the surf roared along the cove and up the cliffs, I would see him in a thousand forms, and with a thousand diabolical expressions. Now the leg would be cut off at the knee, now at the hip; now he was a monstrous kind of a creature who had never had but the one leg, and that in the middle of his body. To see him leap and run and pursue me over hedge and ditch was the worst of nightmares. And altogether I paid pretty dear

for my monthly fourpenny piece, in the shape of these abominable fancies.

But though I was so terrified by the idea of the seafaring man with one leg, I was far less afraid of the captain himself than anybody else who knew him. There were nights when he took a deal more rum and water than his head would carry; and then he would sometimes sit and sing his wicked, old wild sea-songs, minding nobody; but sometimes he would call for glasses round, and force all the trembling company to listen to his stories or bear a chorus to his singing. Often I have heard the house shaking with 'Yo-ho-ho, and a bottle of rum'; all the neighbours joining in for dear life, with the fear of death upon them, and each singing louder than the other, to avoid remark. For in these fits he was the most overriding companion ever known; he would slap his hand on the table for silence all round; he would fly up in a passion of anger at a question, or sometimes because none was put, and so he judged the company was not following his story. Nor would he allow anyone to leave the inn till he had drunk himself sleepy and reeled off to bed.

His stories were what frightened people worst of all. Dreadful stories they were; about hanging, and walking the plank, and storms at sea, and the Dry Tortugas, and wild deeds and places on the Spanish Main. By his own account he must have lived his life among some of the wickedest men that God ever allowed upon the sea; and the language in which he told these stories shocked our plain country people almost as much as the crimes that he described. My father was always saying the inn would be ruined, for people would soon cease coming there to be tyrannised over and put down, and sent shivering to their beds; but I really believe his presence did us good. People were frightened at the time, but on looking back they rather liked it; it was a fine excitement in a quiet country life; and there was even a party of the younger men who pretended to admire him, calling him a 'true sea-dog', and a 'real old salt', and suchlike names, and saying there was the sort of man that made England terrible at sea.

In one way, indeed, he bade fair to ruin us; for he kept on staying week after week, and at last month after month, so that all the money had been long exhausted, and still my father never plucked up the heart to insist on having more. If ever he mentioned it, the captain blew through his nose so loudly, that you might say he roared, and stared my poor father out of the room. I have seen him wringing his hands after such a rebuff, and I am sure the annoyance and the terror he lived in must have greatly hastened his early and unhappy death.

All the time he lived with us the captain made no change whatever in his dress but to buy some stockings from a hawker. One of the cocks of his hat having fallen down, he let it hang from that day forth, though it was a great annoyance when it blew. I remember the appearance of his coat, which he patched himself upstairs in his room, and which, before the end, was nothing but patches. He never wrote or received a letter, and he never spoke with any but the neighbours, and with these, for the most part, only when drunk on rum. The great sea-chest none of us had ever seen open.

He was only once crossed, and that was towards the end, when my poor father was far gone in a decline that took him off. Dr Livesey came late one afternoon to see the patient, took a bit of dinner from my mother, and went into the parlour to smoke a pipe until his horse should come down from the hamlet, for we had no stabling at the old 'Benbow'. I followed him in, and I remember observing the contrast the neat, bright doctor, with his powder as white as snow, and his bright, black eyes and pleasant manners, made with the coltish country folk, and above all, with that filthy, heavy, bleared scarecrow of a pirate of ours, sitting far gone in rum, with his arms on the table. Suddenly he – the captain, that is – began to pipe up his eternal song:

'Fifteen men on The Dead Man's Chest –
Yo-ho-ho, and a bottle of rum!
Drink and the devil had done for the rest –
Yo-ho-ho, and a bottle of rum!'

At first I had supposed 'the dead man's chest' to be that identical big box of his upstairs in the front room, and the thought had been mingled in my nightmares with that of the one-legged seafaring man. But by this time we had all long ceased to pay any particular notice to the song; it was new, that night, to nobody but Dr Livesey, and on him I observed it did not produce an agreeable effect, for he looked up for a moment quite angrily before he went on with his talk to old Taylor, the gardener,

on a new cure for the rheumatics. In the meantime, the captain gradually
brightened up at his own music, and at last flapped his hand upon the
table before him in a way we all knew to mean – silence. The voices
stopped at once, all but Dr Livesey's; he went on as before, speaking
clear and kind, and drawing briskly at his pipe between every word or
two. The captain glared at him for a while, flapped his hand again,
glared still harder, and at last broke out with a villainous low oath:
'Silence, there, between decks!'

'Were you addressing me, sir?' says the doctor; and when the ruffian
had told him, with another oath, that this was so, 'I have only one thing
to say to you, sir,' replies the doctor, 'that if you keep on drinking rum,
the world will soon be quit of a very dirty scoundrel!'

The old fellow's fury was awful. He sprang to his feet, drew and
opened a sailor's clasp-knife, and, balancing it open on the palm of his
hand, threatened to pin the doctor to the wall.

The doctor never so much as moved. He spoke to him, as before, over
his shoulder, and in the same tone of voice; rather high, so that all the
room might hear, but perfectly calm and steady:

'If you do not put that knife this instant in your pocket, I promise,
upon my honour, you shall hang at the next assizes.'

Then followed a battle of looks between them; but the captain soon
knuckled under, put up his weapon, and resumed his seat, grumbling
like a beaten dog.

'And now, sir,' continued the doctor, 'since I now know there's such a
fellow in my district, you may count I'll have an eye upon you day and
night. I'm not a doctor only; I'm a magistrate; and if I catch a breath of
complaint against you, if it's only for a piece of incivility like tonight's,
I'll take effectual means to have you hunted down and routed out of
this. Let that suffice.'

Soon after Dr Livesey's horse came to the door, and he rode away;
but the captain held his peace that evening, and for many evenings to
come.

Robert Louis Stevenson
from *Treasure Island.*

Windjammer

Boat bow cuttin' water
Salt spray flyin' over me head,
Canvas flappin' in de wind
An' lanyard rattlin' ah song.
De mast like two tree growin',
An' de boom swingin' away.
Watch yu arse or yu head gone.
An' is up an down, up an down
In an' out, in an' out,
An' de water makin' green
An' de wave look like mountain
Swish-swishing an' foamin', mutterin'
Like dey makin' conversation,
An' foam all roun de boat like soap
An' ah wish to god ah did stay home.
Who sen' me eh? who sen' me?
No shade on de deck,
Sun bussin' me skin,
Ah bound to peel,
An' me done so black already.
If yu ever catch me puttin' foot
On any kind ah boat again, yu lie.
Is alright for dem sailor an dem
Eatin' bluggoe an 'saltfish,
An talkin' bout how is ah calm day.
If dis is calm, well, Jesus help,
Ah wouldn't want to see it rough.
Dem seasick pills don't work neither...

(*bluggoe*: a kind of fish)

Paul Keens-Douglas

The bridge

Out of the silence grows
An iron thunder – grows, and roars, and sweeps,
Menacing. The plain
Suddenly leaps,
Startled, from its repose –
Alert and listening. Now from the gloom
Of the soft distance loom
Three lights and, over them, a brush
Of tawny flame and flying spark –
Three pointed lights that rush,
Monstrous, upon the cringing dark.
And nearer, nearer rolls the sound,
Louder the throb and roar of wheel,
The shout of speed, the shriek of steam;
The slope of bank,
Cut into flashing squares, gives back the clank
And grind of metal, while the ground
Shudders and the bridge reels –
As, with a scream,
The train
A rage of smoke, a laugh of fire,
A lighted anguish of desire,
A dream
Of gold and iron, of sound and flight,
Tumultuous roars across the night.

J. Redwood Anderson

Night mail

This is the night mail crossing the border,
Bringing the cheque and the postal order,
Letters for the rich, letters for the poor,
The shop at the corner and the girl next door,
Pulling up Beattock, a steady climb –
The gradient's against her but she's on time.

Past cotton grass and moorland boulder,
Shovelling white steam over her shoulder,
Snorting noisily as she passes
Silent miles of wind-bent grasses;
Birds turn their heads as she approaches,
Stare from the bushes at her blank-faced coaches;
Sheepdogs cannot turn her course,
They slumber on with paws across;
In the farm she passes no one wakes
But a jug in a bedroom gently shakes.

Dawn freshens, the climb is done.
Down towards Glasgow she descends
Towards the steam tugs, yelping down the glade of cranes
Towards the fields of apparatus, the furnaces
Set on the dark plain like gigantic chessmen.
All Scotland waits for her;
In the dark glens, beside the pale-green sea lochs,
Men long for news.

Letters of thanks, letters from banks,
Letters of joy from the girl and boy,
Receipted bills and invitations
To inspect new stock or visit relations,
And applications for situations,
And timid lovers' declarations,
And gossip, gossip from all the nations,
News circumstantial, news financial,
Letters with holiday snaps to enlarge in,
Letters with faces scrawled on the margin.
Letters from uncles, cousins and aunts,
Letters to Scotland from the South of France,
Letters of condolence to Highlands and Lowlands,
Notes from overseas to the Hebrides;
Written on paper of every hue,
The pink, the violet, the white and the blue,
The chatty, the catty, the boring, adoring,
The cold and official and the heart's outpouring,
Clever, stupid, short and long,
The typed and the printed and the spelt all wrong.

Thousands are still asleep
Dreaming of terrifying monsters
Or a friendly tea beside the band at Cranston's or Crawford's;
Asleep in working Glasgow, asleep in well-set Edinburgh,
Asleep in granite Aberdeen.
They continue their dreams
But shall wake soon and long for letters.
And none will hear the postman's knock
Without a quickening of the heart,
For who can bear to feel himself forgotten?

W. H. Auden

Killer whale

Looking at the characters

There are four main 'characters' in this story: the storyteller, George, the Reverend Kinnear...and the whale.
Read the story again and find out as much as you can about each of them. Make up charts like this to record what you find:

Looking at the language

1   This story is set on the coast of Fife, in Scotland. It uses a number of dialect and specialist words. Make a list of them and explain what you think they mean.
    If a word is completely unknown to you, look carefully at the sentence it is in and try to work out what it must refer to.
2   The language of the story is poetic and makes considerable use of images. For example the whale is described as 'a black boomerang'. This is because of its shape and because it leaps out of the sea into the air and returns to the same place. Pick out three more images and, for each of them, describe the picture you get in your mind when you read it.

Character : George

What it says in the story	My comments
...the pages of his bible fluttered in the blue breeze...	He is a religious man.
'Is it like the ones you used to hunt for?'	He used to be a whale hunter.

Thought banding

There is more about still images and thought banding on pages 134-135.

A   1   Choose a key moment from the story.
    2   Make a still image based on that moment.
    3   Thought band that moment: let each character speak his or her thoughts.

B   Repeat this process for other key moments. Then use the ideas you have built up as the basis of an improvised play, or a written story.

The old sea-dog

Working on the clues

Like many openings of novels this one gives you clues as to what might be going to happen but it also creates a number of mysteries and puzzles.

Here are some of them:
1   From what is the old seaman hiding?
2   For what does he keep looking each day?
3   Who is the man with one leg?
4   What is in the chest?

Writing

What do you think happens next? Use your ideas about the clues to help you work out the next part of the story. (If you already know the story, make up an incident that happens to the old sea-dog, but which is not in *Treasure Island*.)

Windjammer

Tone

An important part of the effect of this poem is the tone of the speaker's voice. Try reading it 'aloud inside your head' – so that you begin to hear that tone.

1   How would you describe the tone?
2   What kind of person do you think is speaking?
3   What effect does the voice have on you?

Dialect and accent

1   Where do you think the speaker comes from?
2   Why do you think this?
3   How does the writer indicate the speaker's accent?
4   How many dialect and non-standard words are there in the poem?
5   What examples are there of non-standard grammar?
6   Choose one sentence from the poem and explain what it would be in Standard English.

The bridge

Thinking points

This poem gives a vivid description of a steam express train – something that nowadays we normally only get the chance to see on film.

1   Which of the five senses does the poem appeal to?
2   For each of the senses you have listed, quote some words from the poem which appeal to that sense.
3   These are some of the words the poet uses to describe the train: roars   leaps   scream
    Why do you think he chooses these words?
4   Can you find any other words in the poem that do a similar thing?

Writing

Write a description of a machine or some other object as if it were alive. Choose your own object and creature for comparison, or take a pair from this list:
hang glider/bat
bulldozer/giant beetle
school buildings/venus flytrap
motor bike/wasp

Night mail

Group reading

This poem was written to be read aloud, as the commentary for a film made by the Post Office. The film showed the journey of a train travelling from London to Scotland and the poem was intended to give the sounds and rhythms of the journey. Prepare a group reading:

1   Choose one section of the poem to work on.
2   Experiment with reading it in different ways to bring out the sounds and rhythms. For example:
●   one person reading it all
●   each line being read by a different person
●   grouping the lines in twos and threes with each group of lines being read by a different person
●   reading some of the lines in chorus (all speaking together)
●   having some people making train noises as a background to parts of the poem
3   Decide on the most effective way of reading your section and practise until you are ready to perform it.

Part B

Using words

Dialect, words and grammar

Remember

Accent is the way in which people from different places pronounce words and sentences.

Dialect is the different form of English used by people from different areas and different groups.

Standard English is the dialect of English that is used when speaking in formal situations and normally when writing. It is the dialect that is understood throughout the English-speaking world.

Dialect in words

The most obvious way to tell one dialect from another is the different words they use for the same thing. What word would you put in the space? On the map you can see some of the words they use in different parts of England.

Dialect in grammar

Dialects also differ in their grammar: in the way in which speakers construct sentences.

Somerset dialect	Standard English
somewhere about	**about**
eight year	eight year**s**
me first lot	**my** first taste (or drink)

Seeing the differences

Now read the story on the facing page. There are several places where the speaker uses grammar that is different from Standard English. (This is called 'non-standard grammar'.)

1 Make a table like the one above.
2 List all the occasions when he uses non-standard grammar.
3 Against each one write the Standard English grammar.

Eating parsley

My first taste of cider, now, that's rather funny, because I wasn't all that old. I was somewhere about...oh eight year old when I had me first lot of cider and I can tell you what happen. We used to go up and we used to tell the farmer's wife, see, 'We'll pick up the eggs, ma'am.' So we used to pick up the eggs purposely to go into the cellar, see? We used to go in these here cellar – brother as well – and we used to have these little coffee bottles – fill them up – down the hatch. And that was marvellous as far as we was concerned.

But what did your mother say when you went home smelling of cider?

Aah but we didn't let hers know that, see. Ooh not on your nelly! No. We used to go in the garden and we used to pick off some parsley and chew it. You know – well 'tis terrible strong stuff like. We didn't like it. Not like we did the cider, but anyway that's what we done. Go in the house. Well, everything was all right until we was going to beed, 'cos we always had to kiss mother goodnight, mind. Didn't matter what happened, you had to kiss her goodnight, otherwise you was for it. And she used to say, 'You been eating that parsley again, William.' Course 'n we couldn't... tell her...?... we'd have a hiding, see?

So anyway that went on for some time and then after we got a bit – you know, left school and all that, and got older, and Mother was dead against drinking, see? So we had to wait till we was – oh I expect I was – ooh thirty, I expect before we told her. For certain. And I said – mother was on about this parsley – and I said, 'Now look here mother,' I said, 'Why we used to eat this here parsley,' I said, 'we used to go up and have a drink,' I said,'out in the cellar,' I said. 'And we had to eat that there, see,' I said, 'So's you wouldn't know we'd had it.' 'Ooh you crafty bounders,' she said – 'cos she never used to swear. She wasn't that type of person.

Dialect stories

The conversation on page 123 is written with normal spelling, although the main speaker was using a local dialect. The printed version does not give a very clear idea of what he sounded like. It is however possible to use spelling to try to show what a dialect sounds like.

The prisoner

Howsivir, the last day o' the last month, the King takes her to a room she'd nivir set eyes on afore. There worn't nothin' in it but a spinnin' wheel an' a stool. An', say he, 'Now me dear, hare you'll be shut tomorrow with some vittles and some flax, and if you hain't spun five skeins by the night, yar hid'll goo off.'

An' away he went about his business. Well, she were that frightened. She'd allus been such a gatless mawther, that she didn't so much as know how to spin, an' what were she to dew tomorrer, with no one to come nigh to help her? She sat down on a stool in the kitchen, an' lork! how she did cry!

Howsivir, all on a sudden she hard a sort o' knockin' low down on the door. She upped and oped it, an' what should she see but a small little black thing with a long tail. That looked up at her right kewrious, an' that said:

'What are yew cryin' for?'

'What's that to yew?' says she.

'Nivir yew mind,' that said. 'But tell me what yew're crying for.'

'That oon't dew me noo good if I dew,' says she.

(Suffolk dialect story)

Working it out

The spelling gives us an idea of what the story should sound like. It also makes it very difficult to read.

1 Try reading it aloud.
2 Try to work out what all the words are meant to be. Most of them are words from Standard English, but you may find some difficult, for example:
   vittles: victuals (food)
3 Now retell the story in your own words. Does it remind you of any story you have heard before?

The story on page 125 was written in North Yorkshire dialect.

1 Try reading it aloud.
2 Work out the meaning of any parts you found difficult.
3 Make a list of any dialect words used. (Words that are not Standard English; **not** words that are just spelled differently.)
4 Find three places where the grammar of the story is different from the grammar of Standard English. Write them down and explain what the grammar of Standard English would be.

Picnic sight

Ah's all fer goin oot fer a drive on t'moors, specially i' Spring when
t'ling's that purple, thoo could clothe Royalty in it.

Hooivver, sum fooaks can't bear ti leave their cars fer even a few
minnits, an' thoo can see 'em all ovver wi' their picnic tables an' chairs
slap bang next ti their cars, even i' laybys bi t'sahd o' t'A1.
Ah hed a freetenin' experience wi' yan o' that sooart yance. Ah's got this
lahtle Morris Minor, thoo sees. Ah were tekkin' sum friends up ti see
t'mooars recently, an' Ah tonned a bit sharpish-lahk inti this car park an'
inti what Ah thowt were a speace.

T'on'y trubble was, there were this family picnicking in it. Mi bumper
jist happened ti catch t'edge o' t'feller's chair an' tipped it a bit. He
gave a shoot an' toppled oot of it, on'y he jist happened ti be poorin' a
cup o' tea at t'tahm. T'tea sooarta left his mug in a girt broon wodge an'
sailed throot'air landin' reet on their Alsatian, which were sleepin' bi
their feet.

T'dog let oot a shriek fit ti wak t'deead, an' took off roond t'car park
lahk a bat oot ov 'ell. Hooivver, its lead were fastened ti t'leg o' t'wife's
chair, an' t'chair went wi' it, wi' t'woman hangin' on fer dear lahf.
Roond an' roond t'car park went t'dog, wi t'chair screechin' alang
behind, an't'woman screechin' even looder. It were lahk t'sleigh scene
fra Doctor Zhivago. Three tahms roond they went, an' then t'lead
snapped. T'dog took off ovver t'Hole o' Horcum, an' as far as Ah knaws,
it's goin' yet. T'chair, wi' t'woman still abooard, cam straight fer ma at
full speed, an' rammed smack inti mi bumper.

Ah gets oot o't'car slowly-lahk, an' walks roond ti lewk at t'damage.
Then Ah lewks at t'woman an' Ah sez, 'Hey, missis, if thoo wants ti
goa joy-ridin' thoo wants to mak sure thi brakes are werkin'.'
By gum ! If lewks could kill, Ah'd hev bin bonnt ti a crisp on t'spot.

Got a problem?

Every time you work together in a group you need to know what you have to do and how you can achieve that.

You may have seen this list of advice for group work before.

1 Which point do you think is the most important?
2 Which point do you think is the least necessary?
3 What kind of things would happen if groups did not follow rules like this?

In a good group:
1 Everyone listens to everyone else.
2 There is one good leader.
3 Everyone understands what is going on.
4 Everybody has a fair chance to speak.
5 There are no quarrels and arguments.
6 The group pauses every so often to check how it is getting on.
7 Decisions are made by agreeing not by voting.
8 Everyone has a chance to be the leader.
9 The group plans how it is going to work before it starts.
10 People do not interrupt each other.

Playing a part

There are many different ways in which you can contribute to a group. Which of these four roles do you think describes you best of all?

Compare what you think about yourself with someone else's view of you. Sometimes, people believe you have abilities that you don't recognise yourself. In what other ways do you contribute to a group? Are they helpful or unhelpful?

1 **The leader**: the person who is full of ideas, pushing the group forward.
2 **The chairperson**: the one who tries to see that everyone has their say and that conclusions are reached in good time.
3 **The developer**: the person who takes an idea and helps the group to improve it.
4 **The compromiser**: the one who tries to get people with very different ideas to come to an agreement for the sake of the group.

Too much of a good laugh

Class 2X have always enjoyed a good laugh and, on the whole, their teachers have not minded because they are also very hard working. But there are problems too. One of them is the student teacher taking them for science. He didn't have much confidence to begin with and now, almost half a term later, his nerves are in shreds. Their normal science teacher has no idea what is going on because she retires to the staff room during the student's lessons.

Several members of 2X wish that it had not gone so far and are worried that their examination results in science will be a disaster. The difficulty is that no one knows how to stop the game, even though it is no longer much fun (because it is so easy). Someone suggested telling their science teacher but others are afraid that the student will then fail his teaching practice because of their behaviour.

On your own

Write down at least one possible solution to this situation.

In a group

1 Share your ideas with one another, seeing if you can improve on any of them.
2 What other ideas can your group come up with?

3 When you have got as many ideas as you can, make a note of the good and bad points about each idea.
4 Finally, choose the best solution. Try to make the choice a unanimous one.

127

Helping hands

When Joanne found the diary in her room she knew that she should just hand it back. After all, Karen had been her best friend for two years and everyone has got a right to their secrets, haven't they? On the other hand, Joanne was curious to know what her friend wrote in her diary. A little look couldn't do much harm, could it? So Joanne opened the diary...and regretted it at once.

Karen's Diary

If you open this your fingers will shrivel and fall off.

YOU HAVE BEEN WARNED!

June 3rd.
Joanne called for me on her way to school as usual. She was late again. Still I wasn't ready either. She's a good friend but I wish she'd grow up a bit.
She's useful mind you. If there are two of you in the shop and one of you looks as innocent as Joanne, it makes the job easier.

June 4th
Stayed behind after school to help Mrs Brendt clean out the aquarium. It was a bit messy but Mrs Brendt seemed pleased. She described Joanne and me as a couple of real helping hands. On the way home, these "helping hands" picked up several chocolate bars. The funny thing is that I don't eat all that much chocolate. I gave two bars to Joanne and she seemed delighted. I don't think she had a clue how I got them. How dumb can you get!

June 5th
Felt ill today. Mum let me miss school. Perhaps I'm allergic to chocolate. Perhaps I just needed a day off.

June 6th
Mary has said Steven wants to invite me out. I didn't believe her but Rachel said it was true so it must be. Mary says that Steven is absolutely loaded because his dad has his own business. Good looking and wealthy! How can I lose? I must get some decent perfume.

June 7th.
Went into Fulfords in town after school today. Joanne didn't want to come but I talked her into it. I got her to ask about some silver earrings whilst I pocketted the perfume. It worked like a dream. On the way home, Joanne said: "All that way into town for nothing." If only she knew.....

Joanne put the diary down at that point because she wanted to think about what she had already read. These were the first thoughts that she had.

> I could still go along with her but say I'm nothing to do with it if she gets caught.

> I could tell Jean who works in the corner shop so that Karen gets caught. She deserves it.

> I could wait outside the shops when Karen is about to shoplift.

Group work

Your group is going to think about the advice it gives Joanne. Quite a bit of this will have to be written down so your group will need a secretary. It may also help to have a leader who can see that everyone is involved in the final decisions and advice.

1 Joanne's ideas. What advice would you give her about each of them? Give reasons for your advice: people are more likely to listen when they can see that something makes sense.
2 When you have completed your advice/ reasons, put Joanne's ideas in order of importance: 1, 2 and 3.
3 Try to agree about this.

4 What other possible answers to Joanne's problem can you think of? Each member of the group should write down at least one idea of their own.
5 Now share your ideas.
6 When you have listened to each other, decide what is good and bad about each idea and make a note of that.
7 Put all the ideas – yours and Joanne's – in order: from the most useful down to the least sensible. Once again, try to agree.

Making up a play

The next four pages show you how to turn a written story into a play. You can also use the same technique with a poem that tells a story. You probably know something about this already. This unit reminds you of all the things that you need to do – and the order in which to do them.

Thinking about the story

1 ▶ Reading

On your own, read the story carefully, and let your imagination work on it. Try to see what is happening in your mind's eye. Think about these things:

1 Who are the people in the story and what are they like?
2 How do they behave towards each other?
3 Where is the story taking place – and exactly what does the setting look like?
4 When is the story taking place? (And how does this affect things?)
5 What are the main scenes in the story?

2 ▶ Talking

Now talk to the other people in your group, and listen to their ideas. Discuss everyone's answers to the questions.

3 ▶ Making a scenario

It's useful to make a scenario. This is just a list of the main points in your scene(s).
It usually contains these points:
Scene number and name
Who: a list of the characters in the scene.
Where: the place where the scene happens.
When: the time when the scene happens. How it begins and how it ends.
Action: the main things that happen.
You should write these things down as clearly and as briefly as possible.

Getting ready

4 ▶ Casting the parts

Now decide who should play each part. Some suggestions:

1 Be fair. Don't always give the best part to the same person.
2 Give people a challenge: it's tempting always to give the part of the strong hero to the biggest boy in the group. Why not let someone else have a go? Why have the male characters always got to be played by boys?
3 If there are more characters than actors, try to work out ways in which actors can 'double' – play two parts. (For example if one character appears only at the beginning of the story and another only comes in at the end, then obviously they can be played by the same person.)

5 ▶ Preparing the setting

Now arrange any furniture you want for the scene. Find any 'props' you need (objects that are necessary for the actors to use). Don't worry about them being realistic – just find things that will represent them.

6 ▶ *Thinking*

When everything else is ready, stop talking and moving about.
Just sit down for a moment and ask yourself some questions about
your character in the story:

1. What am I like?
2. What are my thoughts and feelings about other people in the story?
3. When do I come into the scene and why?
4. When do I leave the scene and why?
5. What important things must I remember to say or do?

Improvising

7 ▶ *Acting*

Now it is time to improvise the story.
Without any more planning or discussion, start
acting out the story, making up the words as you
go along. Some suggestions:

1. Keep going. Don't stop just because one or
   two small things don't go quite right. You can
   sort them out later.
2. Keep in character. Don't be tempted to stop
   being the Goodwife and be yourself again.
3. Help the other actors. If you can see someone
   is starting to get stuck (eg lost for words) try
   to find a way of helping them out. (But keep
   in character.)
4. Concentrate on the story.

8 ▶ *Discussion*

When you have finished, talk about how the scene went.
Think about these things:

1. Did it tell the story in the way that you wanted to?
   (Or did it get off the point?)
2. Did it tell the story in a way that an audience would have understood?
3. Did the characters turn out right? (Did they speak and behave as they
   should have done?)
4. Did the scene flow (or were there times when it got stuck and people
   were lost for words)?

As you answer these questions try to think of ways in which the scene
can be improved.

9 ▶ *Polishing*

Now is the time to start polishing up your scene.
The discussion should have shown you where it
needs more work. Either run through the whole
scene again or just do those parts of it that need
most practice. After each piece of acting, stop
and discuss again what you have done and where
you are going.

Performance

10 ▶

When there is no more to talk about and no more
to improve (or when there is no more time!) then
you are ready to show your scene to an audience.

Get up and bar the door

It fell about the Martinmas time,
    And a gay time it was then,
When our goodwife got puddings to make,
    And she's boiled them in the pan.

The wind so cold blew south and north,
    And blew into the floor;
Quoth our goodman to our goodwife,
    'Get up and bar the door.'

'My hand is in my household work,
    Goodman, as ye may see;
And it will not be barred for a hundred years,
    If it's to be barred by me!'

They made a pact between them both,
    They made it firm and sure,
That whosoe'er should speak the first,
    Should rise and bar the door.

Then by there came two gentlemen,
    At twelve o'clock at night,
And they could see neither house nor hall,
    Nor coal nor candlelight.

'Now whether is this a rich man's house,
    Or whether is it a poor?'
But never a word would one of them speak,
    For barring of the door.

The guests they ate the white puddings,
    And then they ate the black;
Tho' much the goodwife thought to herself,
    Yet never a word she spake.

Then said one stranger to the other,
    "Here, man, take ye my knife;
Do ye take off the old man's beard,
    And I'll kiss the goodwife.'

'There's no hot water to scrape it off,
    And what shall we do then?'
'Then why not use the pudding broth,
    That boils into the pan?'

O up then started our goodman,
    An angry man was he;
'Will ye kiss my wife before my eyes!
    And with pudding broth scald me!'

Then up and started our goodwife,
    Gave three skips on the floor:
'Goodman, you've spoken the very first word!
    Get up and bar the door!'

Group work

Now follow the instructions in the flowchart opposite and dramatise the
poem. Don't worry about saying exactly what each of the characters said,
but put it into your own words. You will need to work in a group of 4 or 5.

1 Read the poem

2 Discuss it

4 Cast the parts

3 Make a scenario

5 Prepare the setting

6 Think about your character

8 Talk about how it went

7 Act the scene(s)

No

9 Polish it

Satisfied?

Yes

10 Ready to perform

Still images

This photograph 'freezes' a moment in time, leaving us with a still image to look at. What do you think is happening?

In drama, we can also create our own still images. We do this by 'freezing' our bodies in the position we would be in at the very moment a camera clicks and captures the action. This can help us to focus on a particular moment in the drama:

- to find out the mood of a character from their expression and posture;
- to explore the relationships of the characters
- to discover things about the characters and situation, which we may otherwise have missed.

Creating a still image

In *Buy Fiddly Hi Fi, Dumb Chum* there is a moment when Ant discovers that his personal stereo has no batteries in it (see page 18). Create a still image based on this. You need to work in a group of about five.

1 Give each member of the group, the part of one of the characters in the play.
2 Discuss what the different characters would be thinking.
3 Discuss how you would show this in a still image.
4 Each member of the group then moves into these positions and 'freezes'.
5 Take it in turns to step out of the image and look closely at the rest of the group. Give suggestions as to how the still image could be improved.
6 When your group is satisfied with your still image, present it to the rest of the class.
7 Discuss the outcome of your image.

Imaging and thought banding

Sometimes, photographs and still images can be deceiving. We cannot always tell what a person in a photograph or still image is really thinking. A person can be smiling, but their thoughts might be angry or sad. Look at these close-up pictures of the faces in the first picture. What do you imagine each of them is thinking?

Obviously, we cannot ask people in a photograph what their true thoughts are, but in a still image, we can find this out by asking the characters what they are thinking. This technique is called thought banding.

Using thought banding

1 Create your own still image/photograph of a celebration, e.g. a christening, a birthday party or a family party.
2 Each character in turn speaks out loud what they are thinking at that exact moment.
3 Move out of the image and discuss any points you feel are important with the rest of the class.

By using thought banding with still images, we can focus on important moments in plays, stories, poems or our own improvisations, and get to know the true thoughts and feelings of the characters.

Using script

Interpretation

It's impossible to 'read' a play! We can **watch** a play, but when we read the words of a play, what we are reading is the **script**. A play only happens when actors use the words of the text to create characters. Before this can happen, the actors must **interpret** the text.
Here is a line from a script.

Helen: There you are.

Without more information, we cannot tell how Helen says this line. Here are some possibilities ...

| Frightened | Happy | Evil | Bored | Excited | Angry |

How do we know which of these ways is the right way? Here are two questions to help us to find out.

1 What sort of person is Helen?
   We can find this out by looking at:
   a) What the playwright tells us about Helen when she first appears.
   b) What Helen says to other people.
   c) What other people say to Helen.
2 What is happening to Helen?
   We can find this out by looking at the stage directions.

Sometimes there is no 'correct' way to interpret a line. Different people will have different ideas and this can make the interpretation of a script more interesting.

You try

1 Get in pairs, **A** and **B**.
2 **A** has to greet **B** using the word 'Hello'.
3 **B** then has to greet **A** with the word 'Hello', but said in a different way (for instance: nastily, sarcastically or suspiciously).
4 See how many different ways you can say 'Hello'.
5 Keep saying 'Hello' to each other until you can't think of any more ways!

The mystery of the disappearing characters

Characters lost in script shock horror!

A group of characters disappeared from a script as it was being published in the Oxford English Programme Book 2.

The writer of the script was at a loss to explain their disappearance. 'I only turned my back for a minute and they were gone,' the writer said.

Police baffled

Detectives investigating the case were unable to decide how many characters had disappeared and who had said which line. They have released the script and have appealed to the public to help them solve the problem. The lines of the script appear below.

*　　*　　*　　*

It's not fair.
What isn't
Everything.
You're always moaning.
Yeah, that's right.
No, I'm not.
You are. Last week you were moaning
about exams, pocket money, your mum and dad
and your hamster going mad!
Is your hamster going mad?
How can you tell?
He doesn't run round his wheel any more,
he goes to the top and jumps off.
He's probably gone mad listening to you moaning
all the time.
Shut up! I don't moan all the time.
Well, what's not fair now?
Pardon?
What's not fair?
Oh. Er, I can't remember ...

Can you help the police?

1　Read the script carefully and decide how many characters are missing.
2　Give the characters names and decide who said what.
3　Act out your version to the rest of the group.

Dramatisation

We can make up a script from a story that we have read or heard. This is called dramatisation. Turn the following story into script.
Improvise it first, then write down the words you have used.

One morning, when Ant is late for school, his mother refuses to make him breakfast as that will make her late too. Louise calls for Ant, but he refuses to go to school until he has had a cup of tea. Louise teases him that boys are hopeless in the kitchen. Ant decides to show her he is not, and makes some tea – but he puts the teabags in cold water in a pan, and puts the pan on the stove to boil. At this point, Marlon and Fatty turn up.

137

Fact and opinion

Thank you very much indeed!

'THE PEOPLE in this bus queue would like to thank you for driving a new Audi.' Thanks, that is, for introducing a catalytic converter to cut down pollution by Audi engines.

Well, here's a very big thank you from this queue of Londoners huddled in wait for a number 141. Thank you Audi and thank you all car makers for your lead-free exhausts and Britain's 22 million cars.

Thank you for London's traffic, which now crawls along at an average speed of 11 mph. Thank you for the thought that, by the year 2000, the average speed in the capital will be 5 mph. And by 2025, when the number of cars on our roads will have gone up by between 83 per cent and 142 per cent, the whole city may have ground to a halt.

By then of course we won't have buses. As more cars make the traffic slower, the bus companies make less money. So we get fewer buses.

So all but the poorest of us will have cars. (Thanks again for them.) Then of course we'll need more roads.

Thankfully Britain is spending £12 billion on new roads that will speed through what used to be beauty spots, and be made from stone quarried out of the heart of the countryside.

Roads along which we can drive faster, and crash more than the once every eight seconds we do now.

Road accidents killed 5,041 people in Britain in 1988. One of them was 12-year-old Kelly Holland. She was waiting for a bus when two vehicles travelling at speed smashed into her.   Thanks a lot !

The Indy 19 October 1989

Looking at the facts

The newspaper report contains two types of 'fact'. There are statements about the past: for example, that new Audi engines contain catalytic converters to cut down fumes. There are also predictions about the future based on statistics: for example, 'by the year 2000, the average speed in the capital will be 5 mph...'

1 Make separate lists of each kind of fact mentioned in the article.

Looking at the opinions

The two sets of 'facts' are used to support the author's opinions.

2 How would you sum up those opinions?

The other side

3 Imagine that you are a car manufacturer. Write a short letter to *The Indy* complaining about this article and putting the opposite point of view.

138

Don't mention the war

'Donner und Blitzen! Vill these Englander schweinhun never give up?'

It may come as some surprise, but the Second World War isn't over yet. It has been re-fought 12 times a month every month ever since 1961, in war magazines called *Battle, War* and *Commando*.

In the stories, the British are always strong and brave. They usually have good, wholesome names like Sergeant Jack Flint. The same cannot, however, be said of the Germans. They have names like 'murdering swine'. And they say things like, 'Achtung, Englander pig-dog,' a lot.

With 1992 and a Single European Market looming, all this talk about nips, wops, frogs and eyeties seems more than a bit out of date.

The only people who still read these magazines, you would think, are gun-crazy boys, still at that age when happiness is a mock shoot-out behind the school bike shed.

Actually, research carried out by *The Indy* shows that the average war mag reader is more likely to be a commuting businessman than a schoolboy.

Fantasy role-play takes the mind off a hard day in the office.

Picture the scene: the odds are stacked against you. Your officer hates you and sends you to take out a machine gun nest.

You end up saving his life and helping British bombers to fly safely over France to obliterate Dresden. After a hard day in the office, what could be better?

Perhaps it might be better to remember that the war ended forty-five years ago, and that Germany rose out of the rubble to become the most powerful nation in Europe. It has the most efficient industry, the biggest Green party, and the largest influence on the Economic Community. The time has come to forgive.

'Murdering German swine' isn't the most useful way of thinking about our partners in Europe.

What the middle aged readers say

- "I lost one of my two brothers during the war. Jimmy was a pilot in the R.A.F. When I read these cartoons, I imagine he is one of the characters."
  (Trevor, 64, retired.)
- "Of course these stories are stupid, of course the drawing is bad. But when you read these cartoons, you are the hero – you are doing exactly what the hero is doing."
  (Richard, 42, salesman.)

- "The foreign characters' faults exaggerated? Not at all. The Germans and the Japanese lost the war and we saved the French. It's normal to have a good laugh at them."
  (David, 54, porter.)
- "I love these stories in which German b*****s are being killed by our army. They get what they deserve".
  (Mike, 45, driver.)

- "I read any war story, so I also read these cartoons. With them, the pictures put you straight into the action. You don't have to create yourself anything, just live the story."
  (Ian, 45, shop assistant.)
- "My wife thinks that I'm crazy. She says these comics are for children."
  (John, 53, city gent.)

The Indy 12 October 1989

What do you think?

When you have read the material on this page, think about the facts and opinions it presents.

1   What do you think of the arguments that are put forward?
2   What are your own opinions of such war comics
    and the people who read them?

An apple a day

They say that an apple a day keeps the doctor away. Is it true – or just an old superstition like not walking under ladders? The next four pages present different kinds of information about apples and other kinds of food and what our bodies do with them.

When researching, we often have to look in a number of different places to find the information needed, and then bring together the facts we have discovered. This unit gives you practice in that.

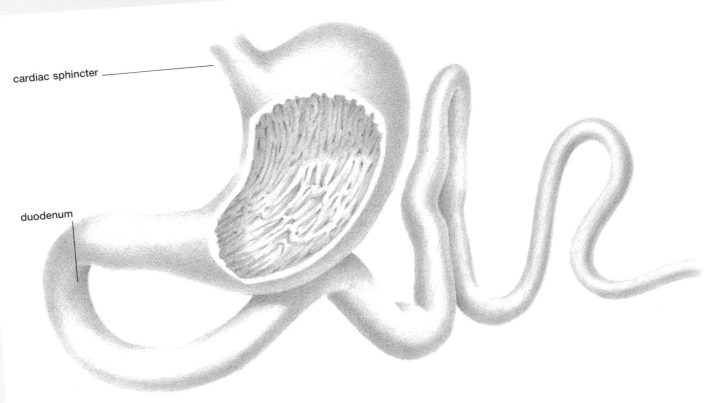

cardiac sphincter

duodenum

The Stomach and Small Intestine

Food is scarcely out of your stomach before it gets a bath of two juices that pour from a hole in the intestine wall. These juices, which come from the pancreas and the liver, combine with the stomach acid and make it less likely to hurt cells that it might touch. Enzymes in the juices chop up fat molecules that are too big to do your cells any good. Now the fat part of your cheese sandwich becomes more useful. Enzymes and juices also pour out of millions of little groups of cells in the intestine wall. They go to work on the protein in cheese and bread. Still other enzymes break up starches and sugars that are left in any vegetables and fruit you ate.

Full of nourishment, this wonderful soup flows slowly through the small intestine. It goes around bends, even uphill once in a while. What keeps it moving? The intestine squeezes and relaxes, somewhat the way the oesophagus does. But movement is helped by tiny waving fingerlike things called villi. Millions and millions of villi line the intestine walls. Each one contains three tubes, two full of blood and one vessel full of a colourless liquid called lymph.

Your cardiac sphincter opens to let food into your stomach from your oesophagus. The three layers of muscles in the wall of your stomach churn the food and mix it with juices that help to digest it. The pyloric sphincter opens to let food move along into the duodenum.

The molecules of starch, sugar, and protein float among the villi. Then suddenly, one after another, they disappear into the blood vessels together with minerals and some of the vitamins in your food. Blood now carries them along on the next part of their journey to nourish your body's cells.

Other vitamins and molecules of fat seem almost to be sucked into the lymph vessels in the villi. We'll catch up with them later on.

The Large Intestine

You may think that by now everything you had for lunch is used up. But there are always some leftovers. They move along, out of the small intestine into a pouch called the cecum at the beginning of a bigger, fatter tube called the large intestine.

Dangling from the cecum is a small tube that looks like a worm. Scientists named this small tube the vermiform appendix. That means 'an extra part in the shape of a worm'. In humans, the appendix seems to be an unnecessary body part. Sometimes the appendix gets irritated and sore. Scientists don't know why this happens to some people and not to others. When doctors remove the appendix, the patient gets along fine without it.

From the cecum, the thick liquid of undigested food is pushed onward. Suppose you had a piece of celery or an apple for lunch. Celery and apples contain little strings called fibre. So does bread made of whole wheat. The fibre is not digested in the small intestine.

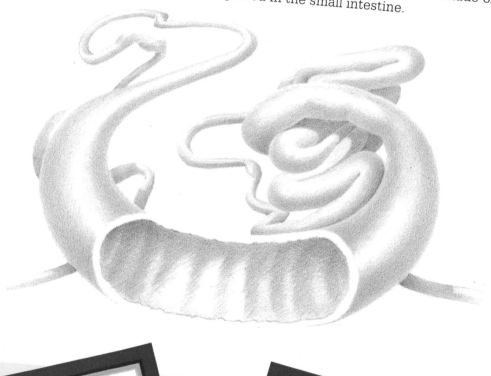

It is recommended this fruit is washed before eating.

N U T R I T I O N

Eating Apples: Apples are a valuable source of Vitamin C. The amount they provide varies from one variety to another but for an average sized apple (150g) it is between 25% and 50% of the recommended daily amount.

AVERAGE COMPOSITION	PER 150g (5¼oz) serving	PER 100g (3½oz)
Energy	302kJ/72kcal	201kJ/48kcal
Fat	0g	0g
	0.7g	0.5g
Protein	18.0g	12.0g
Carbohydrate	3.0g	2.0g
Fibre		

THIS PACK CONTAINS APPROX 6 SERVINGS BY WEIGHT. THE NUMBER OF APPLES MAY VARY.

I N F O R M A T I O N

Packed for Tesco Stores Ltd, Cheshunt, EN8 9SL. © Tesco '90.

TESCO
COX
APPLES
A FULL FLAVOURED
TRADITIONAL VARIETY
Class 1

The average weight of a Cox's apple is 100g.

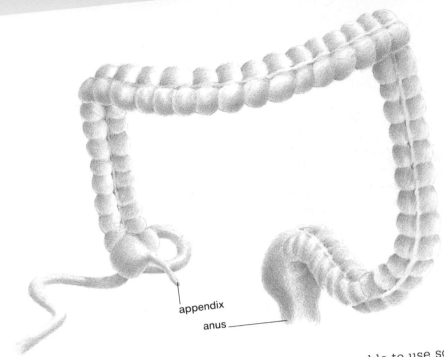

appendix

anus

However, bacteria that live in your large intestine are able to use some of these leftovers. They digest some fibre and other substances and turn them into food for themselves. They also turn some of the food material into vitamin K. Your body then uses this vitamin to make other substances that stop the blood flow when you cut yourself. At the same time the bacteria produce waste materials of their own. One of them is gas.

A great deal of gas develops in the intestine when bacteria digest a certain kind of sugar in beans. Pressure from a lot of the gas may sometimes cause a sharp pain. (The gas doesn't smell very good either.) Can you guess why airplane pilots in World War II, during the 1940s, were forbidden to eat beans? In an airplane high above the earth, the outside air pressure on the body decreases, so

Questions

Look at all the extracts on these four pages. Where would you find information about each of the following topics? (For some of them you will find information in more than one place.)

1 Apples
2 What the appendix is
3 Fructose
4 Villi
5 Enzymes
6 What fibre is
7 Why we need to eat fibre
8 What happens when we eat apples
9 Fat
10 The duodenum

Writing

1 Choose two of the topics and make a list of all the information you can find out about them in this unit.
2 For each of the topics, write one of the following, based on your list of information:
● an explanation to be included in a children's encyclopaedia
● an explanation that is suitable for a bright 5 year-old

'Does an apple a day keep the doctor away?'

Crunching an apple won't mend a broken leg or cure a bout of the measles, of course; but apples *are* good for you and help to keep you healthy, for a number of reasons.

First they are a natural food which contain a large amount of what is called fibre or roughage. Lots of food fads that suddenly interest adults (and some doctors) are little more than just that – fashions. However, the recent trend in the Western world towards a high fibre diet is a good one. Many of the under-developed countries already have diets full of fibre, and they have largely avoided some illnesses which are quite common in the West.

One of the main benefits of a high fibre diet is that the bowels work much better on bulky food which has not had all the natural roughage taken out. In the past, when the expression 'An apple a day' was first used, people realised that fruit like the apple helped to prevent constipation, although they didn't have all the scientific knowledge we have now. Instead of believing it to be the effect of the fibre, they thought raw apple juice helped the breakdown of food in the intestine.

'My granny says that green apples will make me run to the toilet.'

One green apple is unlikely to. However, fruits do contain various sugars, such as glucose, fructose and sucrose. Both green and ripe apples (and pears incidentally) contain a lot of this one called fructose. If too much of this gets loaded too quickly into the first part of the bowel it can't cope. So the partly digested food is moved quickly on to the second part. This can cause belly ache and make you run to the toilet.

Another reason is that apples are high in fibre. This also speeds up the passage of the apple through you.

It is only recently that the limitations of the bowel in dealing with fructose have been realised. It has been known for a long time, though, what fruit can do to your insides. In the days before apples were imported they would suddenly become available at one time of the year when the home-grown crop was picked. Some greedy people ate too many too soon. Then they suffered for it.

Follow-up

The two extracts on this page come from a book called *Can you get warts from touching toads?* In it a doctor answers a number of questions that young people often ask, such as:

- Do poisonous mushrooms only grow under trees?
- Is it true you shouldn't drink from the hot tap?

You can find out the answers to these questions by looking at the right book in the library.

1 What kind of book would you need for each of these questions?
2 Where in the library would you find it?

When you have decided on the answers to those questions, see if you can find answers to the questions opposite about mushrooms and drinking water using your school or local library.

History in words

Language does not stay still. New words are born and old words die. Words also change their meanings as time passes.

What to do

Each box illustrates 3 or 4 meanings for a common word in use today. Some of them are still true, but others have died out. For each box:

1 Make sure that you understand all of the meanings illustrated.
2 Give a short explanation of each meaning.
3 Explain how the meaning of the word has changed.
4 Try to explain why you think it has changed.

Shampoo

A shampoo in the 1700s

A shampoo in the 1800s and later

A shampoo in the late 1900s

Swap

Two meanings of 'swap' in the 1300s

'Swapping' in the 1400s

In the 1900s

I'll swap my knife for your.

Pretty good, eh?

The word 'pretty' has changed its meaning since it was first used in Old English, over a thousand years ago. These made-up sentences show how it has changed.

Old English (prœttig):
He's a pretty fellow: he waited until I was asleep and then he changed his dirty old boots for my new ones. That was a pretty thing to do.

1300s:
a) It was a pretty idea to use two old barrels to get across the river when the bridge was broken.
b) Mark is a pretty man: there's no one braver or more handsome in the whole town.

1400s on:
Everyone in the village thought Helen was a pretty girl: there was no one as good-looking as her this side of Lincoln.

144

What do you call the...er...you know what?

Sometimes people are embarrassed to use a particular word for something. So instead of doing so, they use a different word which they think will be less embarrassing or 'offensive'. Such words are called 'euphemisms'.

How would you complete the question in each of these situations:

- when speaking to a friend, whose house you are visiting for the first time
- when speaking to someone your own age at a school you are visiting for the first time
- when speaking to a teacher at a school you are visiting for the first time
- when in a strange town you ask a traffic warden

Where do the words come from?

The language we speak today is based on Old English, which was spoken in the centuries before the Norman Conquest. Not one of the words we use for the...er you know what comes from Old English: The boxes on this page illustrate how those words developed.

1 Look at the information.
2 Work out how the words 'toilet', 'lavatory', 'WC' and 'loo' got their present meanings.
3 Explain in your own words how and why each word got its present meaning.

Lavatory

A lavatory in the 1600s

A lavatory in the 1300s

Toilet

In the 1500s

In the 1600s

A lady at her toilet in the 1700s

American toilet in the 1800s

Privy

People used to call a toilet a 'privy'. This word comes from the French *privé* which means 'private'.

WC stands for water closet. The word closet used to mean a cupboard or a small private room. The word originally came from French.

The word 'loo' has a possible source in the French phrase *lieu d'aisance* meaning 'place of ease'.

English and proud of it!

Where English words come from

She is right. Hamburgers are named after the city of Hamburg in Germany and the word tomato originally came from the language of the Nahuatl Indians in Central America. They called the fruit 'tomatl' and the European explorers in the Sixteenth century changed this to 'tomate', which they found easier to say. Bananas were brought to Europe by Spanish explorers travelling from the coast of West Africa. The word comes from one of the languages of that area. Of course, the two girls were sitting in a café, which comes from the French word for coffee.

More words

Many English words come from other world languages. Often a study of where the words come from will tell us a lot about history.

On the facing page are two tables of words: one to do with food and eating, the other concerning clothes and materials. The words are listed in the first column. There are three other columns: **Col. 2** is a blank column for meanings. **Col. 3** is a column for the languages the words originally came from (and sometimes the original word).
Col. 4 is a column for additional information about the words.
The information in columns 3 and 4 has been jumbled up.

What to do

1 Copy out the table and fill in the words in column 1.
2 Work out the meanings (or look them up, if you are not sure) and fill in column 2.
3 Work out what ought to go in columns 3 and 4 and fill them in too.

Column 1	Column 2	Column 3	Column 4
Food			
apricot		Arabic: al-birquq	Arabic for roast meat
avocado		Arabic: kabab	from restaurer=restore
casserole		Aztec: xocolatl	It comes originally from a Greek word pitta=cake
chocolate		Caribbean Indian word: batata	Originally from the German word Kuchen=cake
chutney		Central American Indian: ahuacatl	
coleslaw		Dutch: koolsla	Short for koolsalade: cabbage salad
curry		French	The French word means froth
kebab		French	The Italian originally meant little cords
menu		French	
mousse		French	
pasta		French	
pizza		Hindi: catni	
potato		Italian	
quiche		Italian	
restaurant		Italian	
spaghetti		Tamil: kari	
Clothing			
anorak		Arabic: mukhayyar	ki=to wear; mono=thing
beret		Arabic: sikkah	Originally from Persian shir o shakkar=milk and sugar
blouson		Eskimo	Originally from the Latin birettim, a cap
boutique		French	
denim		French	The Arabic word means choice. In English it became mocayare, before changing to its present form
jeans		French	Nîmes was where the cloth came from
kaftan		French: de Nimes	
kimono		Hindi: sirsakar	
mohair		Italian: Genoa	
seersucker		Japanese	
sequin		Turkish: qaftan	

True or False?

1 The word barbecue came from Spanish. The Spanish got it from the Caribbean, where it originally meant a framework of sticks.
2 Bikinis are named after Bikini atoll where the first atom bomb was tested. They got the name because when they were first worn they caused as much of a disturbance as an atom bomb.
3 Leotards are named after Jules Leotard, a French acrobat.

Skewered

Andrew hoped that Victor would come round and see him on Friday but instead he saw Victor's mother turning in at the gateway. Andrew ran into the kitchen to warn Mum.

'Mrs Skelton's coming up the path,' he said. 'She's coming to see us.'

Mum was leaning over the side of the playpen, handing Edward a piece of bread and butter. He took it in both hands and twisted it in opposite directions like a man tearing up phone directories.

'Coming to see us?' said Mum. 'Or coming to inspect us? Do we get a certificate when she's been?' Mum had heard about Mrs Skelton's housekeeping.

Andrew could hear feet crunching on the gravel at the side of the house. He looked round the kitchen for something to put away and decided to fold up the ironing board. As he propped it against the wall he noticed that Ginger had been walking along it with muddy paws, leaving a trail of pussyfoot prints from one end to the other.

Mrs Skelton was at the back door. Mum was still wrestling with Edward. As she backed away from the playpen he reached up with buttery fingers and grabbed the knot of hair at the back of her neck.

'Buttered bun,' said Andrew. Hairpins dropped out and it unrolled into a long skein with Edward swinging on the end. Mrs Skelton knocked.

Mum rolled up her hair again and drove a skewer through it to keep it in position.

'That's not funny,' said Andrew, seeing the skewer. Mum opened the door and looked down, suddenly. Victor's mother only reached her shoulder.

'Come in, Mrs Skelton,' said Mum. Andrew dodged into the living room, leaving the door open so that he could hear what was going on.

'I'm looking for Victor,' said Mrs Skelton. 'I thought he might have dropped in here.'

'I haven't seen him today,' said Mum. 'Do sit down? Won't you have some coffee?'

There was a thump as Victor's mother sat down.

'I won't stay for coffee, thank you,' she said.

I bet she's afraid of catching something from our cups, thought Andrew.

'Victor seem to come here rather a lot,' said Mrs Skelton. 'I hope he's no trouble to you.'

'No trouble at all,' said Mum. 'No trouble to me, anyway. We like to see him. Besides, he's only been here two or three times.'

'I should think that seem a lot,' said Mrs Skelton. 'It do him good to go about with your Andrew. He don't have many friends. He's a bit backward.'

You old boot, thought Andrew.

'I wouldn't call Victor backward,' said Mum. 'He doesn't seem backward to me. From what Andrew tells me he's very knowledgeable about aircraft. And gorillas. He's very well up on gorillas.'

'What good will that do him?' said Victor's mother, peevishly. 'I think you've got something caught in your hair, at the back, Mrs Mitchell.'

'It's a skewer,' said Mum. She didn't explain why it was there. Andrew wondered if she was embarrassed and doubted it. A chair scraping on the floor told him that Mrs Skelton was getting up to go. Perhaps she was afraid that Mum would whip out the skewer and run amuck. When he heard the door close he went back into the kitchen.

'Eavesdropper,' said Mum. 'What a strange person. She didn't look at me once. She kept staring over my shoulder. What could she have been looking at?'

'The ironing board, I expect,' said Andrew, pointing to the row of footprints along the middle of it.

Mum looked at them admiringly. 'That's neat,' she said. 'That's very neat. You know, we could make a fortune flogging that pattern as trendy wallpaper.'

Jan Mark
from *Thunder and Lightnings*

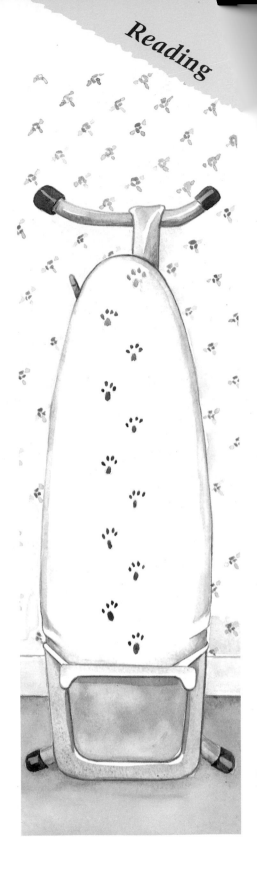

149

First impressions

Before looking in any great detail at what Jan Mark has written, jot down
some first impressions of the characters in this story.
Make up a chart like this:

Characters:	First impressions
Mrs Skelton Victor Mrs Mitchell Andrew	

Taking a closer look

First impressions are sometimes misleading. The way to check them is to
look carefully at the evidence there is about the characters. Although Jan
Mark's book is basically about Andrew and Victor, this section
concentrates on their mothers. Think about the differences between them
and make up a table like this:

	Andrew's mother	Victor's mother
Her attitude to the home		
Why you think this		
Her attitude to Victor		
Why you think this		
Her attitude to awkward situations		
Why you think this		

Looking back

How would you revise your first impressions in the light of your further
thinking about the passage and the mothers in particular?

Thinking again

You should now have a fairly good impression of the two mothers' characters. You may also have noticed how Jan Mark does not tell us very much about what they look like. That is left to the imagination. Try to build up a picture of the two mothers. Jot down all the ideas you can think of about:

● their face
● their hair
● what they normally wear
● what they normally cook
● how they behave with their husbands
● what they do in their spare time

Think about how you might complete these sentences for either of them:

● If she is annoyed by something she...
● If a baby was sick on a carpet, she...
● If her husband was late for dinner, she...
● If her son wanted to stay at a friend's house for the weekend, she...

Writing

Use all the ideas you have built up to write a detailed description of the two mothers.

Another conversation

Andrew and Victor have gone plane spotting and have promised to be home by 5.00 p.m. It is now 5.15 p.m. and there is no sign of the boys. Mrs Skelton has just rung Mrs Mitchell's doorbell. Imagine the conversation that occurs.

Write out the conversation: *either* as a script (see page 180) *or* as direct speech (see page 181).

151

The way that you say it

Father/Mother: Where on earth have you been until this time? You're late again.

Son/Daughter: I'm sorry, but ...

Father/Mother: Sorry! Sorry! Coming in at this time of night and all you can say is 'sorry'?

Son/Daughter: If you'll let me explain ...

Father/Mother: Explain? There is nothing to explain. You're late. You were told to be back by nine, and for the umpteenth time this month you're late. Well, that's it. Enough is enough. You've been warned and you've taken no notice. You've gone too far this time: you're grounded for six weeks.

Son/Daughter: But it won't happen again.

Father /Mother: I know it won't happen again. You won't get a chance. Your routine is fixed from now on: tea, homework, bed. Have you got that? Tea, homework, bed.

Son/Daughter: But what about the Duke of Edinburgh?

Father/Mother: The Duke of Edinburgh's not my problem. But if he gets home as late as you do then he should be grounded as well.

In pairs

1 Read through the scene above, and then perform it as you think it should be spoken. There are no stage directions. The style of the writing makes the tone clear.

2 The mood of each of the three pieces of dialogue below is less clear. Choose one of the pieces of dialogue, and make up a situation in which the lines are spoken.

Let me go

Say this in three different ways, to give the following meanings:
a) I beg you to give me permission to go;
b) please choose me for the errand;
c) take your hands off me.
If you were successful in conveying the different meanings, how did you do it?

David is here

Say this three times. The first time stress the first word; the second time stress the second word; the third time stress the third word. What three meanings did you convey?

Inflection

In everyday speech we convey meaning by the way we say things. We would normally speak the following sentences with a rising tone of voice. Try them out, and explain the mood that is conveyed in each case.

> Quick, the train's already in!
> It's an emergency!
> This is the best book I've ever read.

Now try these sentences, this time lowering the tone of your voice. Again, say what moods are conveyed.

> Isn't it dark?
> I've tried, but it's hopeless.
> Come in very quietly.

By changing the tone of voice, we can convey different moods, when speaking the same words. Say the following sentences, first raising the tone of your voice, then lowering the tone of your voice.

Explain the different moods you convey by changing the tone.

> Are you there?
> This is a comfortable chair.
> Come back!

When reading, raising and lowering the tone of voice can emphasise contrasts in the writing. Read the following lines, raising and lowering the tone of your voice in turn, to bring out the contrasted thoughts.

> It was the best of times, it was the worst of times;
> it was the age of wisdom, it was the age of foolishness;
> it was the season of Light, it was the season of Darkness;
> it was the Spring of hope, it was the Winter of despair;
> we had everything before us, we had nothing before us.

153

The way that you write it

Description

The boy was about Oliver's own age, but he was one of the queerest-looking boys he had ever seen. He was snub nosed, flat-browed, and as dirty a juvenile as one would wish to see; but he had about him the airs and manners of a man. He was short for his age, with bow-legs, and sharp, ugly eyes. He wore a man's coat which reached nearly to his heels.

1 What are we told of the boy's size?
2 What was unusual about his eyes?
3 Would a boy or a man usually be 'snub nosed' and 'flat-browed'?
4 What is meant by 'airs and manners'?

5 What sort of things might be meant by the 'airs and manners of a man'?
6 Can you sum up why Oliver thought 'he was one of the queerest-looking boys he had ever seen'?

Sentences

And Aunt Jessie was a wet blanket! She met him with a dark face. He knew as soon as he saw her that something was wrong. She was dressed for fettling. When things were going well, Aunt Jessie took to housekeeping easily; a flick and a run and an occasional scrubbing brush did all she needed. But when the world was against her she took it out of No. 6 Megson Street. She put on her uniform; a sackcloth apron, a duster round her hair, a pair of formidable boots; and she assembled her weapons; buckets and soft soap, hard brushes and soft brushes, carpet sweepers, carpet beaters, and on the kitchen range, every pan in the house boiling away, offering its steamy incense to her mania for duty. What she did seemed not to matter. She had been known to take down every curtain in the house and give them all a glorious communal boiling in the copper, lace curtains and velvet curtains and chintz curtains pellmell, so that all came out marvellously inter-married and with a carefree sharing of racial traits and colours. She had been known to shift every stick of furniture from the front bedroom to the back bedroom; to take up all the carpets and drench the floors beneath them with water that took weeks to evaporate.

1 In the first 5 lines there are 6 short sentences. In the remaining 10 lines there are only 4 sentences. Why do you think the writer mainly uses long sentences in the second part of the passage? Can you suggest why short sentences were used early on?
2 'Fettling' is a dialect word. From the rest of the passage, can you work out what it means? Do you have a local dialect word which means the same thing?

154

I was staying at the time with my uncle and his wife. Although she was my aunty, I never thought of her as anything but the wife of my uncle, partly because he was so big and trumpeting and red-hairy and used to fill every inch of the hot little house like an old buffalo squeezed into an airing cupboard, and partly because she was so small and silk and quick and made no noise at all as she whisked about on padded paws, dusting the china dogs, feeding the buffalo, setting the mousetraps that never caught her; and once she sleaked out of the room, to squeak in a nook or nibble in a hay loft, you forgot she had ever been there.

This is a description of the writer's aunty.

1 What creature is she like?
2 What other words and phrases are used to tell
   us that she is 'small and silk and quick'?
3 Why does the writer include a description of
   his uncle in a passage about his aunty?

Repetition

We are very fond of pineapple, all three of us. We looked at the picture on the tin; we thought of the juice. We smiled at one another and got a spoon ready.

Then we looked for the knife to open the tin with. We turned out everything in the hamper. We turned out the bags. We pulled up the boards at the bottom of the boat. We took everything out on to the bank and shook it. There was no tin-opener to be found.

Then Harris tried to open the tin with a pocket knife, and broke his knife and cut himself badly; and George tried a pair of scissors, and the scissors flew up and nearly put his eye out. While they were dressing their wounds I tried to make a hole in the thing with the spiky end of the hitcher, and the hitcher slipped and jerked me out between the boat and the bank into two feet of muddy water, and the tin rolled over, uninjured, and broke a tea-cup.

Then we all got mad. We took that tin out on the bank and Harris went into a field and got a big sharp stone, and I went back into the boat and brought out the mast, and George held the tin and Harris held the sharp end of his stone against the top of it, and I took the mast and poised it high up, and gathered up all my strength and brought it down.

It was George's straw hat that saved his life that day.

1 Which word appears most often in
   paragraph 1? (The same word is repeated in
   paragraph 2.) What is the purpose of this
   repetition, do you think?
2 Look at paragraph 3, which begins 'Then
   Harris ...' Are there any examples of
   repetition here?

3 In paragraph 2, why does the writer give
   every action a separate sentence? But in
   paragraph 4, from 'We took that tin ...', why
   is every action included in one sentence, do
   you think?
4 What happens between the end of paragraph 4
   and the beginning of the last paragraph?

The Eco Rap

The words and pictures on these two pages come from a TV interview with a young group of musicians who made a rap record about the environment. Their story was told in their own words and there were also captions. The people interviewed were two members of the group, MC Blink and MC Scientist, and Keith Peck of Wide Open Communications, the project organiser.

Caption: ● ● ●7 kids known as New Frontier got together to make a rap record about the environment... ● ● ●

Song
So we are the New Frontier
Rapping for the world, so listen here –
No ozone layer means big trouble
Take care of the air
Or you're living in a bubble

MC Blink: well the record is about the environment/ its called the eco rap big trouble/its telling you about the ozone layer – and – it tells you about the whole world

Keith Peck: at the moment theres seven members of the – of the group – but new frontier are – are actually a sort of a – changing group of children/were looking to reintroduce different children into the concept because what we really want to get out of new frontier is a sort of a movement/more kids that care about the environment

MC Blink: I like mc duke – public enemy – big daddy k – (His voice fades to background and mixes with the song.)

Caption: ● ● ● The kids love rap but have also become aware of ecology through making the record... ● ● ●

Caption: ● ● ● Their mums and dads are having to be more careful what they buy to avoid upsetting the kids!!! ● ● ●

MC Scientist: we want people to know and know that theyre doing the wrong things and everything they should doing is stop chopping down trees/stop – stop digging underground spoiling the earth cos its just like going into a park like hyde park and theres a beautiful green area and digging up a hole in it and leaving – and leaving it and theres nothing and a big pile of dirt next to it/thats how it was like

156

MC Blink: when people are little they copy the big ones so the big ones got to show something first to let the younger ones know like the parents they should tell – be telling the children and they should in – ive noticed in the heart of london in westminster they've got so many dustbins and bottle banks but in lon – in brixton like they havent got hardly any and they should start introducing them here/the money to do the recycling isnt too much because once you recycling youre not using up new resources/youre using the same up/and when you use recycled paper its easier to write on

Song

> *Now what we need is education*
> *For all us kids from every nation*
> *The time has come it's up to us*
> *To take a stand to make a fuss*
> *'Cos the environment was heaven sent*
> *Was given to us by no government*
> *Wasn't meant for abuse by industry*
> *It was given to us for eternity*

MC Blink: mankind have just not been on this earth/like the dinosaurs have been on this earth and they died as well/and thats going to happen to us if we don't do something quickly right – we can/ not tomorrow but today

MC Blink: ⎫ (together) its cool to care
MC Scientist: ⎭ trash is cash

Transcript

The words above are called a transcript: they are the actual words spoken without any punctuation. Instead of punctuation these marks are used:

/ means a natural break or change in the speech (like starting a new sentence in writing.)
– means a pause or hesitation

Reading

Read the transcript aloud. Try to make the spoken words sound as much like natural speech as you can.

Writing

Now look carefully at the first two pieces of speech (from MC Blink and Keith Peck.) Write each one out putting in punctuation, but not changing any of the words or leaving any out. What are the difficulties in doing this?

What's the difference?

Apart from the lack of punctuation, how could you tell that this material is a transcript from speech? Think about these things:

1 The words they used.
2 The way the sentences went.
3 How each speech was organised.
   (Did they organise what they had to say in the same way as we organise things when we are writing? If not, what is the difference?)

Newspaper report

Use the information on these two pages as the basis for a newspaper report on the formation of New Frontier and the release of *The Eco Rap – Big Trouble*.

Wish you were here

15th July 1990

Dear Nan and Grandad,
We arrived in Norwich on Saturday and went straight to the houseboat on the River Yare. It's about four miles outside Norwich. The boat is really comfortable and it's fun getting up in the morning to the sound of the lapping river. Mum and Dad send their love and say they'll be writing soon. Hope you are both well and Nan has recovered from her cough.

Best wishes,
Jennifer xx

Dear Alex,

15th July

I'm missing you a lot and thinking about you all the time. The days are just dragging and I can't wait until Friday to get back on the train and come home. Hope you'll be able to be at the station – the train gets in at 6.35 pm. I hope your exams have gone well this week – I'm only sorry I wasn't there to help you revise (and things!) I just wish I could be with you now. It's been miserable here. Hope you're missing me.

All my love,
Jen xxxxxxxxxxxx

Dear Emma,

15th July – You really made the right choice in not coming on this 'holiday'. It's been raining nearly all the time and Mum and Dad have been grumpy with each other (and me). The loo got blocked up this morning and this young bloke came to fix it. I had to stay in to wait for him. The ducks have driven me crazy.

BORED!

Quack, quack,
QUACK QUACK xxx Jenny

QUACK QUACK

Thinking about the postcards

1 Read Jennifer's three postcards carefully.
2 Think about how her writing changes depending on her audience: both what she says, and how she says it. Think about these points:
   a) Are there things she tells some people and not others? If so, what?
   b) Why do you think this is?
   c) Are her attitudes and opinions different in different cards? If so, how?
   d) Why is this?
   e) What other differences can you see?

158

15th July 1989
Dear Diary,

What a day. An early morning family row, a blocked loo, and Peter. I feel so muddled up. Can you love two people at the same time? I really miss Alex and I'm looking forward to seeing him again. But I met Peter today and that's changed things for me. I bet M + D wouldn't have left me this morning if they'd thought the bloke coming to fix the loo would be a handsome 17 year old! The son of Mr Vernon, the owner of the boat yard. Bet he's filthy rich – though he didn't have a car. I don't know, why did I agree to see him again tomorrow? It can only complicate things. What a mess. Aargh.

Thinking about the diary

Sometimes a piece of writing is for no audience other than the writer. When we write notes, jottings, shopping lists, or diary entries, it is often for our eyes only. The fact that no one else sees it will sometimes influence the way we write it. In what ways does Jennifer's diary entry differ from the three postcards? Think about both the content and style of the writing.

Writing as Jennifer

Imagine you are Jennifer and the holiday is over.

1 Write a letter to Peter.
2 Write a diary entry.
3 Describe the ways the audience has affected the writing of the two pieces.

Writing as Peter

Imagine you are Peter.

1 Write a short letter to Jennifer.
2 Write a letter to her parents (Mr and Mrs Rosen) reminding them they have not paid the bill for unblocking the boat's toilet.
3 Describe the ways the audience has affected the writing of the two pieces.

159

Purposes for writing

Writers write for a reason! Their writing has a purpose. Some important purposes for writing are shown below.

argue
describe
persuade
ask questions
solve problems
narrate
show you understand
inform
explain
amuse
protest
reflect
brainstorm
predict
entertain
express feelings
record
try ideas out
sort things out
order

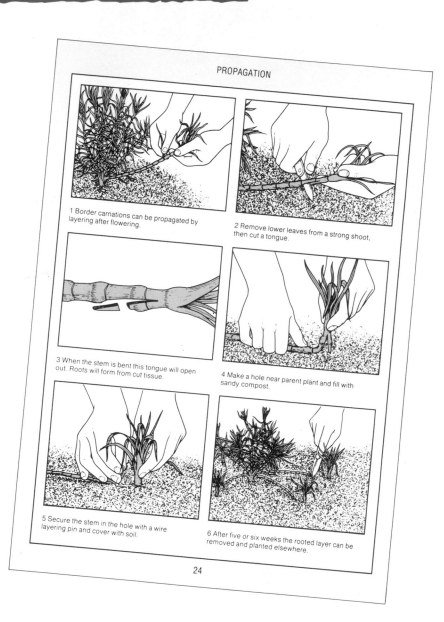

PROPAGATION

1 Border carnations can be propagated by layering after flowering.

2 Remove lower leaves from a strong shoot, then cut a tongue.

3 When the stem is bent this tongue will open out. Roots will form from cut tissue.

4 Make a hole near parent plant and fill with sandy compost.

5 Secure the stem in the hole with a wire layering pin and cover with soil.

6 After five or six weeks the rooted layer can be removed and planted elsewhere.

24

Thinking points

1 Most pieces of writing have more than one purpose although they may well have one that is more important than the others. Study the four texts on these pages and try to work out the possible purposes for each. Back up your ideas by quoting from the text.

LOSS OF TRADITIONAL COUNTRYSIDE

For every tree which is chopped down, up to 6 more are planted in its place. The trouble is that these new trees tend to be specially developed strains which are often alien to the areas in which they are planted. What is more, they are planted at high density – equivalent to about 20 on an average sized modern suburban building plot – and sometimes in places where trees should not grow at all. All this has resulted in the loss of traditional countryside and valuable wildlife habitats.

RECYCLED PAPER

WHAT CAN WE DO?

We can cut down on paper production and waste by, wherever possible, using re-cycled paper instead. The greater the demand for re-cycled paper, the lower the production and the wastage of new paper. Energy usage for the manufacture of re-cycled paper is 40% less than that of 'new' paper. At **Tesco** you can buy **100% re-cycled paper products** (see the list on the back of the leaflet and look out for the special symbol on packs). We are also using more and more re-cycled paper in the packaging of Tesco products and for the leaflets and signs we produce.

As most of the pulp used to produce soft tissue products comes from North America and Scandinavia, we can save on imports as well.

We can also **save** more **paper** for re-cycling. For some years at Tesco, we have been collecting the boxes in which our products are delivered to stores and some of the paper that we use in our offices for re-cycling. We hope soon to introduce 'paper banks' at some of our larger stores to allow you to save your paper waste for re-cycling. Meanwhile, why not find out if your local council or a local charity has a paper collection scheme?

In cases where it is preferable to use new paper, such as coffee filters and sanitary products look for paper which has not been bleached with chlorine gas.

Remember, every little helps!

Aerosol art

From Mr Boyd Hill

Sir: After reading about the youth worker arrested in the graffiti and aerosol art clampdown (23 October), I came to the conclusion that the only way to stop these senseless arrests would be to provide, for what I can see are talented kids, paint sites where they can practise their art.

Street art is a problem for the police and those in authority but for these artists it is often the only means of escape from a society which condemns them for everything they do. It is a pity that in return for all their creativity they receive only a criminal record and huge fines.

Yours sincerely,
BOYD HILL
Street Art Creations
23 October

THE PLEASURE OF PINE

When Judy Wetherby and her husband, Paul, moved into their ground-floor flat in north London, it had already been extended at the back to provide a light, spacious conservatory-style kitchen. New units were needed, however, and they decided on a custom-made kitchen in old pine by Eden Grove Kitchens. Everything was built specially to order, using antique pieces of pine rescued from a variety of different sources.

For all the splashbacks and worksurfaces Judy chose Vert Mexico and Cerises tiles from the Les Hurets range from Tile Mart, which contrast well with the mellow pine. The white oven, microwave and hob are all by Bosch.

One wall is entirely of glass and the two end walls have been painted white, so as much light as possible is let into the room. Plants flourish in this atmosphere and, along with Judy's eclectic collection of china, they add just the right amount of colour and contrast to the room.

Text: Linda Parker

Photography: Tony Timmington

In pairs

2 What other purposes does writing sometimes fulfil? Look through
● the examples given above
● your own writing
● your school text-books
● a magazine or newspaper
Make your own chart of Purposes for writing, listing all the purposes you have thought of.

Writing

1 Choose three purposes for writing from the list opposite. Write three texts, each to fulfil a different purpose. Share your writing with a friend. See if they can guess your three purposes.
2 Choose another three purposes. Try to construct a text which satisfies all three purposes. Share your writing with a friend and see if they can guess your three purposes.

161

Different ways of writing

Writing formats

On your own

Scan the various newspaper and magazine cuttings on these pages. Make a list of the different writing formats you can identify (e.g. advertisements, charts, editorials, reports).

In pairs

Compare your list with a partner's. Can you think of other formats which might appear in newspapers? Look through a whole newspaper together, noting the range of formats used. Try to think of reasons why some formats are more suitable for certain types of information than others. In what ways, for example, does a weather report differ from an editorial?

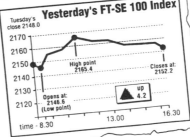

LIGHT FOR EUROTUNNEL

MARKET REPORT

the project's planned £500m rights issue run headlong into the Government's late November privatisation of the electricity companies, the "discos".

Their flotation will soak up about £5bn from the pool of cash available for equity investment, which could hit Eurotunnel.

Over the last year, the shares have plunged from a peak of nearly £12, and yesterday were on the slide again -- down 7p at 438p.

Down at the tunnel face, the English and French boring teams advancing towards each other should break through in November.

Other shares took a breather from the Gulf fiasco. The FT-SE 100 Index closed at 2152.2, up 4.2 after an earlier rally of over 17 points.

Sterling bounced back with a leap of over 2 cents to $1.89 as mounting speculation that the US Federal Reserve Bank is about to cut interest rates to stimulate the economy left the American currency reeling.

Gold climbed over $4.75 to $387.25 an oz. **Oil** for October delivery rose nearly $1 to $29.25 a barrel with September oil spilling over $30.

Buyers were out for oil shares. **Enterprise**, on hopes of an upgrading of its Nelson field in today's interim statement, jumped 10p to 678p. **Burmah**, also with results today, added 4p to 515p.

A share buy-in at **Kleinwort** pushed its price to 330p, up 7p. But leisure giant **Brent Walker** came under attack, down 11p at 169p. **Leading Leisure** climbed 5p to 18p. Talks underway may lead to an offer.

Bulmer was up 2p at 171p following a green light from the MMC on its Frampton Village cider deal.

Yesterday's FT-SE 100 Index

Tuesday's close 2148.0

High point 2165.4
Closes at: 2152.2
Opens at: 2146.6 (Low point)
up 4.2

time - 8.30   13.00   16.30

Daily Express

Opinion

Sir Robert i off the rails

AT least one important aspect Sir Robert Reid's criticism Government transport policy on the mark. As he sugge there has been a lamentable lack of s tegic thinking about the road and networks this country will need once Channel Tunnel is built and the si European market in operation.

Once plunged into this compet world, we run the risk of being behind by countries whose leaders seen the need to eliminate, or at prevent, bottlenecks.

Nevertheless, customers of Br Rail will be tempted to believe the going chairman protests too much explaining his own organisation's ciencies.

Sir Robert complains that BR di get enough money from the taxp But if the corporation had emp greater business aggression and i nation it could have raised signific more cash from its considerable estate assets than it has managed s

In any case, late, dirty, overcro and food- and drink-free trains a solely the result of alleged lack of investment.

vanti: the blues 36 Style **Judy Rumbold: a soft sell in washed silk** 37 Obituary **Eva Turner: the empress of the stave** 21

MediaGuardia

Today's weather forecast

Morning *Afternoon* *Night*

UP & DOWN THE CITY ROAD

...are on the eve of the Broadcasting evolution! From Monday Mr Rupert Murdoch will start transmitting four new television channels to earth from his new outpost in space. Overcome with excitement about the advent of Sky Television, I skipped down to my local television... this week to order a... disappointed...

this time one subservient to commercial interests, was about to take to the air, with the certain result that culture would be relegated to the dustbin – or at least to the middle of the night – as the two channels embarked on a ratings war that would drag them both down into the gutter. In short, it will be for Danes the end of civilisation as they know it.

Oh happy breed that has survived in

High flier Hazel

THE TIMES CITY DIARY

Gilts lose their gloss
Of the three women and four men laid off by Baring Broth-

TV Mail PAGE 21

Miami's vice?

THE SUN SAYS
Keep your noses out

KENYA

TAKE A WALK ON THE WILD SIDE
FROM **£399**

Out now, the new Kenya Summer '91 brochure from Airtours. Holidays from only £399 for two weeks (see brochure page 18). Safari options also available in Kenya and NEW Tanzania. Pick up a copy at your local travel agent today.

AIRTOURS
TEL 0706 260000

AIRTOURS PLC
ALL HOLIDAYS ARE SUBJECT TO AVAILABILITY

School formats

List the different formats of writing you have used in school in the past month. Make a chart of the subjects you study (like the one below) and list the formats used in each one.

1 Does your own writing offer the same range of formats as the daily newspapers?
   Are certain formats used in some subjects but not in others?
2 Can you think of reasons for this?
3 Discuss your findings with a partner.

HISTORY	FRENCH
essay	maps
notes	jokes
diagrams	cartoons
plans	exercises
charts	descriptions

163

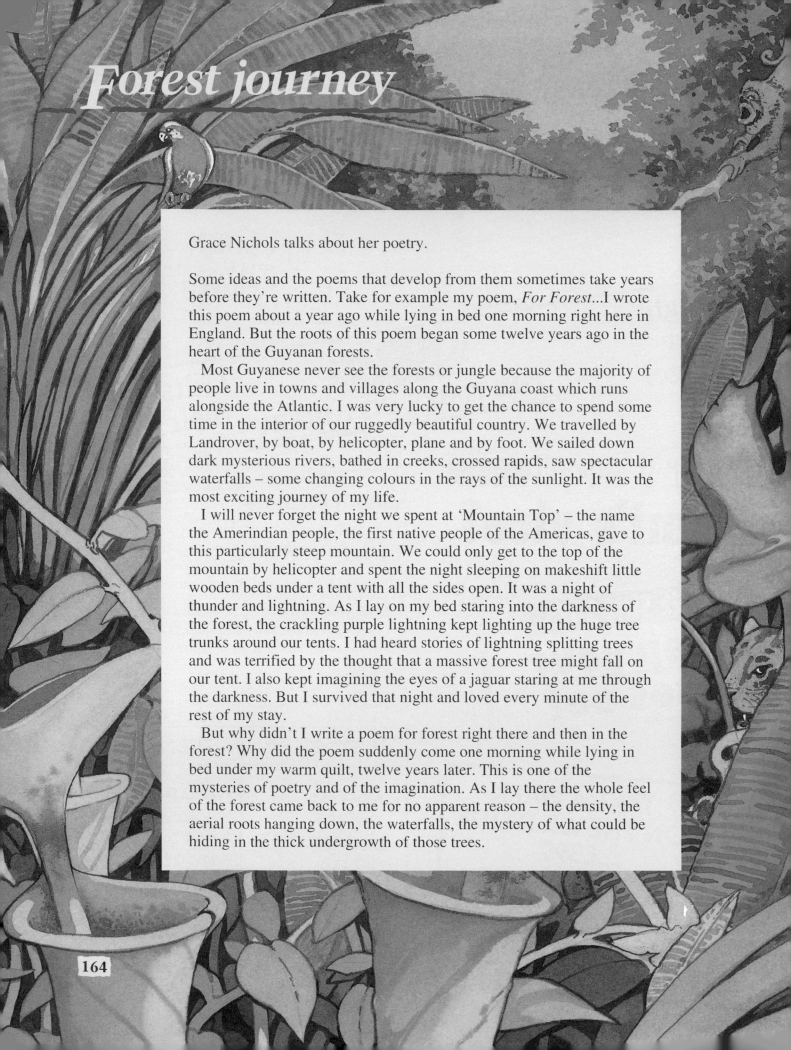

Forest journey

Grace Nichols talks about her poetry.

Some ideas and the poems that develop from them sometimes take years before they're written. Take for example my poem, *For Forest*...I wrote this poem about a year ago while lying in bed one morning right here in England. But the roots of this poem began some twelve years ago in the heart of the Guyanan forests.

Most Guyanese never see the forests or jungle because the majority of people live in towns and villages along the Guyana coast which runs alongside the Atlantic. I was very lucky to get the chance to spend some time in the interior of our ruggedly beautiful country. We travelled by Landrover, by boat, by helicopter, plane and by foot. We sailed down dark mysterious rivers, bathed in creeks, crossed rapids, saw spectacular waterfalls – some changing colours in the rays of the sunlight. It was the most exciting journey of my life.

I will never forget the night we spent at 'Mountain Top' – the name the Amerindian people, the first native people of the Americas, gave to this particularly steep mountain. We could only get to the top of the mountain by helicopter and spent the night sleeping on makeshift little wooden beds under a tent with all the sides open. It was a night of thunder and lightning. As I lay on my bed staring into the darkness of the forest, the crackling purple lightning kept lighting up the huge tree trunks around our tents. I had heard stories of lightning splitting trees and was terrified by the thought that a massive forest tree might fall on our tent. I also kept imagining the eyes of a jaguar staring at me through the darkness. But I survived that night and loved every minute of the rest of my stay.

But why didn't I write a poem for forest right there and then in the forest? Why did the poem suddenly come one morning while lying in bed under my warm quilt, twelve years later. This is one of the mysteries of poetry and of the imagination. As I lay there the whole feel of the forest came back to me for no apparent reason – the density, the aerial roots hanging down, the waterfalls, the mystery of what could be hiding in the thick undergrowth of those trees.

For forest

Forest could keep secrets
Forest could keep secrets
Forest tune in everyday
To watersound and birdsound
Forest letting her hair down
to the teeming creeping of her forest-ground
but Forest don't broadcast her business
No, Forest cover her business down
from sky and fast-eye sun
and when night come
and darkness wrap her like a gown
Forest is a bad dream woman
Forest dreaming about mountain
and when earth was young
Forest dreaming of the caress of gold
Forest rootsing with mysterious Eldorado
And when howler monkey
wake her up with howl
Forest just stretch and stir
to a new day of sound
but coming back to secrets
Forest could keep secrets
Forest could keep secrets
And we must keep Forest

Reading back the poem I was surprised at the line, 'And we must keep Forest' because, in a way, it reflects my own concern about the preservation of our forests. But I didn't set out to say this at all in my poem. I wasn't thinking of making people aware of the importance of keeping our forests. It just came out in the poem. This is what makes poetry exciting for me. A poet can discover things in her own poetry. It's like going on an adventure. You don't know quite where the poem will take you because it has a living mind or spirit of its own. So one of the most important things in writing a poem is to tune in to the feelings of the poem, to listen to that still small voice in the poem, instead of forcing it to say the things you think you ought to say.

Grace Nichols

Thinking about the journey

1 Why did Grace Nichols feel lucky to be making her journey?
2 What did she see during her trip?
3 What do you think was the most memorable moment for her?

Thinking about the poem

1 What is unusual about the way the poem came to be written?
2 Was the poem what you expected after she had described her journey into the forests of Guyana?
3 Were you as surprised at the way that the poem ended as Grace Nichols was?
4 Why do you think it ends like that?

Talking about the forest

1 If you had been lucky enough to join Grace Nichols in Guyana, what would you have liked and disliked most of all?
2 If you were living permanently in a tropical rain forest, what would be the main advantages and the main problems?

The forest speaks

When Grace Nichols writes about the forest, she sees her as a person. Take a look at these two openings. Who do you think is speaking in each one?

There are no secrets
To be kept from her
As she strikes the night with
light,
Splitting sky,
Splitting tree...

His eyes stare out
From between the trees;
He is silent
Amongst the chatter of the forest
But he is watching....

See if you can write about Grace Nichols' journey into the Guyanan forest as if you were one of the creatures of that forest. You don't have to say which creature you are, although your readers may like to guess.
As you begin to prepare this, you may find it helpful to think about Grace and her friends in these ways:
● how they travelled
● what they did
● what they saw
● what happened on the mountain
If writing the first lines is a problem for you, you might like to begin like this:

I am the eyes of the forest
I saw...

Four ways into a poem

There a hundreds of ways in which you might try to write a poem.
Here are just four of them. Try any of these suggestions but be willing
to change if your first idea is not working.
Remember that poetry does not always rhyme but it is constantly seeking
out new ways to say things.

Coming alive

Writing as if a forest or an animal or a building
or a machine could speak to us.

Taking a title

Sometimes a title comes last, sometimes it is
the beginning of a poem.
Grace Nichols calls her poem *For Forest*
but there are plenty of words and phrases in
her poem that would also make excellent titles
for other poems.
Choose a word or phrase from *For Forest*
as a title to start your own writing.

Finding a key line

Grace Nichols says she was surprised at the line
'And we must keep forest,' because it sums up
something very important to her.
Try adapting this line for yourself:
We must keep...
and then build up a poem round it.

Repeating the word

In Grace Nichols' poem, the word Forest
is repeated and it becomes a kind of chant that
runs through the poem. Almost always, it is at
the start of a line. Choose a word of your own
that you think might work in that way. It could
be an object, such as Forest or Ocean or Cat,
but you might also like to think of ideas, such
as Kindness or Believing or Love.

Syllable poems

Poems often work by making patterns. One kind of poem pattern is based on the number of syllables there are in each line. If you aren't sure about syllables, check the explanation on page 191.

Haiku

Haikus come originally from Japan. A haiku is a poem that has three lines. Each line has a fixed number of syllables.

> Tiger – eyes dark with
> half-remembered forest night,
> stalks an empty cage.
>
> *Judith Nicholls*

Line 1: 5 syllables   Ti ger – eyes dark with

Line 2: 7 syllables   half-re mem bered for est night,

Line 3: 5 syllables   stalks an emp ty cage.

Because haikus are so short, you have to focus on just one thing – it's like taking a snapshot of the subject. You haven't got many words to play with, so you have to make every one count.

1 Choose a topic for your haiku.
2 Concentrate all your thoughts on it.
3 Try to see your subject in your mind.
4 Describe it vividly – and briefly.
5 Then change it around to fit the pattern.

Cinquain

Cinquains have five lines, and have their own syllable pattern for each line.

> Hearing,
> The sea rolling,
> Breaking onto the rocks
> Creating foam and a thin surf
> That roars.
>
> *Simon Wiltshire*

Line 1: 2 syllables   Hear ing,

Line 2: 4 syllables   The sea roll ing,

Line 3: 6 syllables   Break ing on to the rocks

Line 4: 8 syllables   Cre at ing foam and a thin surf

Line 5: 2 syllables   That roars.

January to December

The warm cows have gone
From the fields where grass stands up
Dead-alive like steel.

Unexpected sun
Probes the house as if someone
Had left the lights on.

Novel no longer
Snowdrops melt in the hedge, drain
Away into spring.

The heron shining
Works his way up the bright air
Above the river.

Earth dries. The sow basks
Flat out with her blue-black young,
Ears over their eyes.

The early lambs, still
Fleecy, look bulkier now
Than their shorn mothers.

In this valley full
Of bird song, the gap closes
Behind the cuckoo.

Fields of barley glimpsed
Through trees shine out like golden
Windows in winter.

Though nothing has changed –
The sun is even hotter –
Death is in the air.

Long shadows herald
Or dog every walker
In the cut-back lanes.

A crop of mist grows
Softly in the valley, lolls
Over the strawstacks.

Meadows filmed across
With rain stare up at winter
Hardening in the hills.

Patricia Beer

Linked poems

This poem is a sequence of haikus about the
months and seasons of the year.
Try writing a linked group of 2 or 3 haikus
(or cinquains) on a topic of your choice.

169

*G*etting the message across

What you write is very important, but so is how you write. People take a lot of notice of presentation: the appearance of written and printed words on the page. If you want to get your message across you need to think about what it looks like as well as what it says.

Layout

It is important to arrange the words on the page so that they are clear and interesting.
For each of the examples above:
1 Draw a diagram to show how the words are arranged.
2 Explain why you think they have been arranged in this way.
3 Do you think this is effective? What are your reasons?

Now you try

These words and pictures have got to be arranged to form an advertisement.
You can change the size of them and you can arrange them on the page in any way you like. How would you do it?

Save the whale!

Please help our campaign by sending a donation to: Save the whale, PO Box 100, Milton Keynes.

In spite of all our efforts, whales are still being slaughtered all over the world.

Big letter...little letter...

Another way of getting your message across is to use the right kind of lettering.

What are the rules for using capital letters in ordinary writing? Without looking them up, write down the rules. Then check them on page 174.

Using large letters in a poster

When you are making up a notice or poster you may decide to use capital letters to emphasise words that you want to stand out.

You can also make the lettering of some words larger to emphasise them.

For Sale nearly NEW ELECTRIC GUITAR complete with amplifier £75

FOR SALE nearly new ELECTRIC GUITAR complete with AMPLIFIER £75

Lettering

When something is being printed, you can choose which typeface you want to use. You can even use different typefaces in different places. (But it is not a good idea to have too many different typefaces. If you do, it just looks a mess.)

1 abcdefghijklmnopqrstuvwxyz

2
abcdefghijklmnopqrstuvwxyz
ABCDEFGHIJKLMNOPQRSTUVWXYZ

3
abcdefghijklmnopqrstuvwxyz
ABCDEFGHIJKLMNOPQRSTUVWXYZ

4
ABCDEFGHIJKLMNOPQRSTUVWXYZ

5
abcdefghijklmnopqrstuvwxyz
ABCDEFGHIJKLMNOPQRSTUVWXYZ

6
abcdefghijklmnopqrstuvwxyz
ABCDEFGHIJKLMNOPQRSTUVWXYZ

Choosing the right one

Different typefaces are suitable for different jobs. Which of the typefaces on this page would be suitable for each of these jobs and why?

● The menu of a restaurant selling exotic food
● A disco poster
● A sign outside a theatre
● The sign outside a fish and chip shop
● Publicity material sent out by a holiday firm

Putting them in the picture

Sometimes writing a series of sentences is not the only way of communicating information.

Illustration

Often a single picture can do the work of hundreds of words.
What is the point of this picture? How effective is it?

Diagram

When you have to explain how something is done, it may be useful to draw a diagram. Sometimes when you buy equipment you may find that there are no words at all in the instructions.
Write a set of instructions explaining in words what this diagram means.

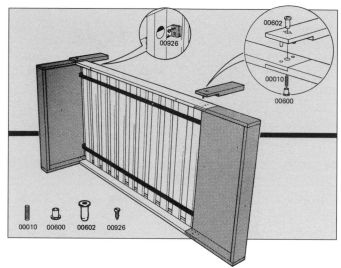

Chart

Information that contains figures is often expressed using a pie chart or bar chart. Explain in words the information expressed in this illustration.

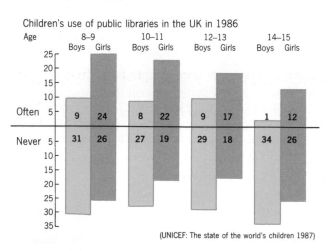

(UNICEF: The state of the world's children 1987)

Question tree

How would you describe a question tree? Explain in your own words what this question tree says.
Make up your own question tree.

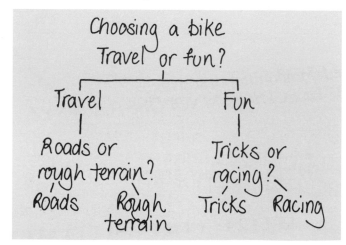

Advertising the disco

They found it difficult to make up the posters.
Here are some of their rough versions:

A

WE ARE HAVING A SECOND YEAR DISCO WITH THE SCREAMING EDBO DISCO. IT WILL COST £1·50 TO GET IN. THERE WILL BE FREE COKE AND CRISPS. YOU SHOULD DRESS UP AS DEMONS AND DRAGONS. IT WILL TAKE PLACE AT 8 P.M. ON THURSDAY 3RD FEBRUARY.

B

SCREAMING EDBO DISCO

£1·50 TO GET IN

FREE COKE AND CRISPS FOR ALL!!

DRESS UP AS DEMONS AND DRAGONS

C

DISCO

8PM 3RD FEBRUARY

FREE COKE & CRISPS!

£1·50

Demons & Dragons

Questions

1 Which of the three gives the most information?
2 Which of them is most clearly set out?
3 Which of them is most eye-catching?
4 Each version has some good points and some bad points. What are the good and the bad points of each one?
5 If you had to choose one of the three, which one would you choose and why?

Making up your own version

Now you try. Use the same information as the three posters, but arrange it in whatever way you like. Don't worry about beautiful lettering or colours at this stage – just arrange the words in the best way possible on the page.

*P*unctuation

Capital letters

Capital letters; are used for these purposes:

1 As the first letter of a sentence.

> Have a nice day.

2 For the personal pronoun 'I'.

> Last week I went to the zoo.

3 At the beginning of a new piece of direct speech. (See page 181.)

> At last he said, 'We won!'

4 For the first letter of proper nouns.

> People's names: Deidre Blackadder
> Places: Brentwood
> Titles of books, plays, films, TVprogrammes:
> > The Oxford English Programme
> Days of the week: Wednesday
> Months of the year: January
> Planets and stars: Jupiter

5 For the first letters of titles of people and organisations.

> Lady Windermere
> Foreign Minister
> Royal Society for the Protection of Birds

6 For initials in people's names.

> W. Shakespeare

7 For initial letters used in abbreviations.

> JP
> IBA
> NSPCC

174

Full stops, question marks and exclamation marks

Normal sentences must end with one of these three marks. . ? !

Statements normally end with a **full stop**.

It is easy when you know how.

A **question** normally ends with a **question mark**.

Do you understand what I mean?

Exclamation marks are used to mark an **exclamation**, or a **forceful statement**.

If only you would listen to what I am saying!

> **Warning!**
> if you use too many
> exclamation marks,
> readers will get
> very tired of them.

Abbreviations

If a word is shortened, or abbreviated, then you usually put a full stop after it.

M.K. Thomas
4.5 kilometres **N.**
Ill. (Illinois)
Col. (Colonel)

There are a number of exceptions to this:

1 Abbreviations made up only of capital letters do not need full stops.

ANC   **OUP**   **FBI**

2 Abbreviations that make up words (acronyms) do not need full stops.

ASH (Action on Smoking and Health)
COSIRA (COuncil for Small Industries in Rural Areas)

3 These abbreviations do not need full stops:

Mr Mrs Ms M (Monsieur) **Mme** (Madame)
Mlle (Mademoiselle) **Dr St Revd**
p (= penny or pence)

Commas

Commas are an important way in which we can make our writing easier to read. A good way to show this working is to turn speech into writing. In *The Eco Rap* on pages 156-157, one of the boys says this:

> when people are little they copy the big ones so the big ones got to show something first to let the younger ones know/like the parents they should tell – be telling the children and they should in – I've noticed in the heart of London in Westminster they've got so many dustbins and bottle banks but in Lon – in Brixton like they haven't got hardly any and they should start introducing them here/the money to do the recycling isn't too much because once you recycling you're not using up new resources/ you're using the same up/and when you use recycled paper it's easier to write on

Dividing it into sentences

The first thing to do is to separate out the sentences. Sometimes this may mean that you have to add or change words:

> When people are little they copy the big ones so the big ones have got to show something first to let the younger ones know. The parents should tell the children. I've noticed in the heart of London in Westminster they've got so many dustbins and bottle banks but in Brixton they have got hardly any and they should start introducing them here. The money to do the recycling isn't too much because once you start recycling you're not using up new resources – you're using the same up. Also when you use recycled paper it's easier to write on.

How many changes have been made so far?

Adding commas

You may have noticed that although it is now easier to read, there are places where it is still a bit confusing:

When people are little they copy the **big ones so the big ones** have got to show something first to let the younger ones know.

I've noticed **in the heart of London in Westminster** they've got so many dustbins and **bottle banks but in Brixton** they have got hardly any and they should start introducing them here.

If we add commas in these places, it makes the sentences easier to read:

When people are little they copy the big ones, so the big ones have got to show something first to let the younger ones know.

I've noticed in the heart of London, in Westminster, they've got so many dustbins and bottle banks, but in Brixton they have got hardly any and they should start introducing them here.

How commas are used

1 In lists.

If a sentence contains a list, then it makes it much easier to sort out what is in the list if we use commas:

In English there are several different punctuation marks, including full stops, apostrophes, commas and inverted commas.

This still applies if the items in the list are each quite long:

He had an interesting collection of old toys: a Victorian doll's house, an early wooden rocking horse, several china dolls and a collection of lead soldiers.

Lists like this usually have 'and' before the last item. Some people say that you should never put a comma before this, but it depends. Sometimes you must put a comma before the 'and'. If you don't, it looks very odd:

> They had a very big menu for their school dinners: spaghetti, stew, salad, fried fish and trifle.

2 Putting things in brackets.

Sometimes when writing a sentence we want to put in something that doesn't belong to the main part of the sentence:

> I've noticed in the heart of London
> **in Westminster** they've got so many
> dustbins...

'in Westminster' doesn't have to be there. The sentence would make sense without it:

> I've noticed in the heart of London
> they've got so many dustbins...

but 'in Westminster' adds useful information. You could put it in brackets

> I've noticed in the heart of London
> **(in Westminster)** they've got so many
> dustbins...

or you use commas instead of brackets.

> I've noticed in the heart of London**,**
> **in Westminster,** they've got so many
> dustbins...

Words used in this way are said to be **in parentheses**.

Apostrophes

Apostrophes are used for two purposes.

1 To show possession (that something belongs to somebody).

2 To show omission (that something has been missed out).

Possession

1 Normally you add **'s.**

> This is the dog**'s** basket, not the cat**'s.**
> This is Maria**'s** book.

2 When the word is a plural ending in **–s**, you just add **'**.

> That is the girls**'** tennis ball.

Notice that these words do not have an apostrophe.

> hers ours yours theirs whose

When **its** means 'of it', you should not put an apostrophe.

Omission

When we are writing informally, or writing speech, we often use
shortened forms. In these cases, the apostrophe shows where the letters
have been missed out.

he is	→	heis	→	he's
they are	→	theyare	→	they're
I do not	→	I donot	→	I don't
it is	→	itis	→	it's

Writing down speech

There are two ways in which you can write down the words that someone says:

1 script

2 direct speech

Script is normally used for plays. Direct speech is most commonly used in stories.

Script

1 The names of the speakers are put in capital letters, on the left hand side of the page.

2 The words spoken are written, without any special punctuation, a little way to the right. The speeches should all start at the same point in the line.

3 Information about an individual character who is speaking, is put in the speech. It is put in brackets and underlined.

4 Information about other things that happen, including sounds and actions is given a line to itself. It is put in brackets and underlined.

GETAFIX: (<u>Singing</u>) Tralala! Tralala!
(<u>ASTERIX</u> approaches him.)
ASTERIX: I'm worried, Getafix. It's a long and dangerous road to the forest of the Carnutes...
GETAFIX: Nonsense!

(<u>GETAFIX</u> begins to move away.)

ASTERIX: (<u>Pleading</u>) Let me escort you, Getafix!
GETAFIX: Asterix, you know quite well that non-Druids aren't allowed at the conference!
ASTERIX: I'll go to the edge of the forest with you and wait for you there...
GETAFIX: Oh, very well. If you insist.

Direct speech

1 Each piece of speech is enclosed between double or single inverted commas.
   In books, single inverted commas are normally used. In school, pupils are often taught to use double inverted commas.

2 Every new piece of speech must begin with a capital letter, even if it is not the first word in the sentence.

3 Each piece of speech must end with a full stop or an exclamation mark or a question mark before the concluding inverted commas...

4 ...unless the sentence is going to continue, when it ends with a comma. This also comes before the concluding inverted commas...

5 When a piece of speech comes in the middle of a sentence it must have a comma (or sometimes a colon) just before the opening inverted commas.

6 For each new speaker you start a new line and indent.

7 When something happens, or there is a sound or you want to describe how someone felt, you just write it as part of the story.

Getafix the Druid, was busy preparing for his visit to the forest of the Carnutes. As he got ready he sang a little song to himself. Then Asterix came up.

'I'm worried, Getafix,' he said. 'It's a long and dangerous road to the forest of the Carnutes...'

'Nonsense!' replied Getafix.

'Let me escort you, Getafix,' pleaded Asterix.

The Druid refused to be persuaded. 'Asterix,' he said, 'you know quite well that non-Druids aren't allowed at the conference!'

'I'll go to the edge of the forest with you and wait for you there...'

'Oh, very well,' said Getafix, 'if you insist.'

Spelling

Ways to better spelling

Nearly everybody finds some spellings difficult. Different people have different ways of solving spelling problems.

Write it down and try it out

Spellings are patterns and our brains are good at remembering patterns. If you aren't sure which of two or three spellings is right, try writing them all out on a piece of paper – which of them looks right?

Use a dictionary

If you think you know how the word starts, look it up in a dictionary. If you aren't sure how it starts, try different versions out on paper first and look them up in the dictionary to find out which one is right.

Look for patterns

English spelling isn't chaotic. Three-quarters of all words are spelled according to a regular pattern. As you are reading and writing, try to be aware of the patterns of letters we use to spell particular sounds.

Look for word families

Words go in families:

```
                ity
author ──────── ise
                isation
```

This family consists of four words. In all of them **author** is spelled the same. **–ity –ise –isation** are spelled in the same way as they are in other words (modernity, modernise, modernisation, for example.)
If you look out for families like this, you will find spelling gets easier.

Learn the rules for changes

Many words have to be changed according to how they are used in a sentence. We have to add bits onto the end of them:

–s/es   one boss...several boss**es**
         I pass...she pass**es**

–ed   She taps...I tap**ped**
         he rakes ... I rak**ed**

–ing   I skated...they are skat**ing**
         I tip...we are tip**ping**

If you learn the rules you will avoid a lot of the mistakes.

These rules are explained on pages 184-186.

Keep a spelling book

Either get a special notebook, or use the back of an exercise book. Write down the words you find difficult, so that you can look them up easily.

Use words

Never be put off from using a new word just because you are not sure how to spell it.

Read books

Read regularly. Reading will not make everyone a perfect speller, but it is difficult to be a really good speller if you never read anything at all.

Making plurals

Plural means 'more than one'.
Most words follow these rules:

1 Normally, just add **–s**.

book	→	book**s**
complication	→	complication**s**

2 Words that end in **–s**, add **es**.

glass	→	glass**es**
genius	→	genius**es**

3 Words that end in **–x** and **–z**, add **–es.**

box	→	box**es**
buzz	→	buzz**es**

But notice : quiz   qui**zz**es

4 Words that end in **–ch** and **–sh**, add **–es.**

branch	→	branch**es**
bush	→	bush**es**

5 Words that end in **–f**, or **–fe** change the ending to **–ve** and add **–s.**

calf	→	cal**ves**
wife	→	wi**ves**

Exceptions

beliefs	chiefs	dwarfs	griefs
gulfs	proofs	roofs	

6 Words that end in **–y**: If the letter before the **–y** is a vowel, just add **–s**.

day	→	day**s**
boy	→	bo**ys**

If the letter before the **–y** is a consonant, change the **y** to **–ies**.

bab**y**	→	bab**ies**
sp**y**	→	sp**ies**

7 Words that end in **–o**: usually just need an **–s**.

piano	→	piano**s**.

Exceptions

A few words add **–es**:

buffalo**es**	mango**es**
cargo**es**	mosquito**es**
domino**es**	motto**es**
echo**es**	potato**es**
go**es**	tomato**es**
grotto**es**	tornado**es**
halo**es**	torpedo**es**
hero**es**	volcano**es**

8 Words that stay the same in the plural:

aircraft	deer	sheep

9 Words that change in a different way:

child	→	children
man	→	men
foot	→	feet
goose	→	geese
mouse	→	mice
tooth	→	teeth
woman	→	women

10 Some Latin and Greek words change in a different way.

crisis	→	crises
formula	→	formulae

Adding –ing and –ed

When we use verbs we have to change them according to the sentence they are in:

I like to **walk** to school. I **walked** to school yesterday, and I **am walking** to school now.

1 Normally you just add **–ing** and **–ed**.

The rules that follow describe the main exceptions.

2 Words with one syllable, with a long vowel, ending in **–e**. Remove the **–e** and add **–ed** and **–ing**.

rake	rak**ed**	rak**ing**
dare	dar**ed**	dar**ing**

But note:

age	ag**ed**	ag**eing**
queue	queu**ed**	queu**eing**

3 Words with one syllable, with a short vowel, ending in a single consonant.
Double the consonant and add **–ed** and **–ing**.

tap	tap**ped**	tap**ping**
beg	beg**ged**	beg**ging**

4 Words with more than one syllable, ending in a single consonant.

If the stress is on the last syllable, double the consonant:

propel	propel**led**	propel**ling**

If the stress is not on the last syllable, just add **–ed** and **–ing**.

benefit	benefit**ed**	benefit**ing**
budget	budget**ed**	budget**ing**
sharpen	sharpen**ed**	sharpen**ing**

5 Words ending in **–l**.

If there is only a single vowel before the **–l**, add **–led** and **–ling**:

compel	compel**led**	compel**ling**

If there is a double vowel before the **–l**, just add **–ed** and **–ing**:

coil	coil**ed**	coil**ing**
peel	peel**ed**	peel**ing**

6 Words ending in **–y**.

If the letter before the **–y** is a vowel, just add **–ed** and **–ing**.

play	play**ed**	play**ing**

Exceptions

lay	→	laid
pay	→	paid
say	→	said

If the letter before the **–y** is a consonant, change the **y** to an **i** before adding **–ed**.

cry	cri**ed**	cry**ing**

185

Adding –ly

We can turn adjectives into adverbs by adding –ly:

He is a quick worker: he works quick**ly**.

Usually you just add **–ly** to the adjective, but there are some exceptions.

1 If the word ends **–ll**, just add **–y**.

full → ful**ly**

2 If a word of two or more syllables ends in **–y**, cut off the **–y** and add **–ily**.

happ**y** → happ**ily**

3 One syllable words ending in **–y** are usually regular.

shy → shy**ly**

Exceptions

gay → ga**ily**
day → da**ily**

Using ie/ei

The rule is: '**i** before **e** except after **c**, when the sound is long **ee**'.

th**ie**f   rec**ei**ve
p**ie**ce   c**ei**ling

Exceptions

s**ei**ze   w**ei**r   w**ei**rd

Using ce/se

The rule is: '**c** for a noun and **s** for a verb'. (Easy to remember because the letters are in alphabetical order: **C Noun S Verb**.)

noun	verb
advi**ce**	advi**se**
practi**ce**	practi**se**
licen**ce**	licen**se**

Example:

I need your advi**ce**: will you advi**se** me?

Words that are easily confused

accept	except	
affect	effect	
aloud	allowed	
bail	bale	
bear	bare	
birth	berth	
board	bored	
chose	choose	
diary	dairy	
great	grate	
heel	heal	
here	hear	
lead	led	
lose	loose	
made	maid	
meter	metre	
miner	minor	
new	knew	
no	know	
pain	pane	
pair	pear	pare
past	passed	
peace	piece	
quite	quiet	
read	reed	
red	read	
right	write	
sew	sow	
some	sum	
stationary	stationery	
steak	stake	
tale	tail	
there	their	they're
threw	through	
to	two	too
wait	weight	
weak	week	
weather	whether	
where	wear	
were	we're	
which	witch	
whose	who's	
wood	would	
your	you're	

Single and double letters

A common spelling problem concerns words with single and or double letters. Here is a list of the commonest:

accelerate	imitate
address	immediate
assist	marvel
harass	mattress
beginning	millionaire
brilliant	necessary
caterpillar	occasion
collapse	parallel
collect	patrol
commit	pedal
corridor	possess
disappear	sheriff
discuss	success
embarrass	sufficient
exaggerate	terrible
happiness	unnecessary
illustrate	woollen

Other problem words

adaptation (not adaption)
adviser
computer
conjuror
connection
conqueror
conscience
conscious
encyclopaedia
forty
grandad
granddaughter
miniature
moustache
rhyme
rhythm
somersault
wagon
yoghurt

Useful words

accent   the way in which a person pronounces words is described as their accent. Everybody speaks with some kind of accent. If the accent belongs to a particular part of the country, it is called a regional accent. People sometimes talk about a 'posh' or 'BBC' accent. This is correctly called 'received **pronunciation**'. Accent is different from **dialect**.

adjective   adjectives work with **nouns**. They help to make the meaning of the noun clearer or fuller. In these examples the adjectives are *marked out*:

> I like reading *exciting* books.
> I'm looking for an *old, green rusty* bicycle.
> Peter is very *happy* today.

adverb   adverbs work with verbs, adjectives or other adverbs. They help to make their meaning clearer or fuller.

> *Working with verbs*:
> He walked *slowly* down the road.
> *Working with adjectives*:
> I am feeling *extremely* happy today.
> *Working with other adverbs*:
> The car came towards her *agonisingly* slowly.

affix   a part of the word that comes before or after the stem or main part. There are two kinds of affix: **prefixes** that come at the beginning of a word; and **suffixes** that come at the end.

apostrophe   see page 179.

argue   to put across a point of view, explaining the reasons why you hold it. For example, 'She argued that the new school uniform was a great improvement on the old, because it was more in line with today's fashions.'

article   the words *a, an, the*.

audience   the person (or people) you are speaking to, or writing for.

autobiography   a biography that someone writes about himself or herself.

biography   the story of a person's life.

borrowing   see **loan word**.

casual (language)   when we are speaking to (or writing for) people we know well, we use **vocabulary** and **grammar** that are less **formal** than when we are speaking to people we do not know well. For example, we might say to a friend 'Hang on a bit,' while to a stranger we would say, 'Wait a minute.'

character   a person in a story poem or play.

clause   a group of words that contains a complete verb and makes sense. These are examples of clauses. (The verb is marked in each one):

> I *hate* coffee ice cream.
> As I *was going* up the stair,
> I *met* a man
> who *was*n't there.

colon   the punctuation mark **:** . It is used to introduce a list, a saying, or a statement.

> 'We only have one rule in this school: treat others as you would like them to treat you.'

comma   see page 176.

command   see **sentence types**.

conjunction   conjunctions are words that join other words together. In particular they join phrases and clauses:

> I like walking along the beach *and* eating ice cream.
> I only saw the bomb *when* I was nearly on top of it.

conversation   when two or more people speak to each other about something. Less formal than a discussion.

description   talking or writing that sets out the main points of something. A description often tells us what something looks or sounds like: for example 'A description of my best friend'. It can also tells us how something works and what the person thinks about it: for example 'A description of that awful school'.

dialect   the form of a language used in a particular area (regional, local dialect), or by a particular group of people (social dialect). Different dialects use different vocabulary and grammar. See pages 122-125.

discussion   a conversation between two or more people about a particular topic. In English and other lessons you will often be asked to 'have a discussion' about a topic.

draft   when we are writing something it often goes through a number of stages: we write it, read it through, think about it and rewrite it or alter it. Each version of the writing is called a draft.

exclamation   see **sentence types**.

exclamation mark   see page 175.

explanation   writing or talking that tells you the how and why of something.

fiction   something that is made up.

first (language)   the language that we are brought up to speak at home. It is sometimes called the mother tongue. For most in Britain this is English, but many have a different first language: for example Gujarati, or Turkish.

foreign (language)   a language that is not generally spoken in a country. People learn it because they want to travel or work abroad. For example, in Britain French and German are foreign languages. Foreign languages are often taught in schools.

formal (language)   when we are speaking to (or writing for) people whom we do not know well, we use language that is formal. We pay more careful attention to the grammar of our sentences and we use vocabulary that we know anyone will find acceptable. See **casual**.

full stop   see page 175.

grammar   grammar tells us how the words of a language are combined to make sentences. In English this is done by *word order* and

changing the form of words:
>   *word order*: 'I saw Peter yesterday.' is an English sentence. 'Yesterday saw Peter I.' is not.
>   *changing the form of words*: the verb 'see' changes to 'saw'. We say 'I saw Peter yesterday.' and not 'I see Peter yesterday.'

graffiti   drawings or messages marked on walls and other public places. They are often obscene; sometimes clever or funny.

image   when a writer wants to describe something vividly, so that readers can see it from different points of view in their mind's eye, he can use an image, a 'snapshot in words':
>   Ants
>   are dragging the wing of a butterfly –
>   See!
>   it is like a yacht.

inverted comma   see page 181.

lecture   When a person talks to a group of people about a chosen subject in a formal way: the lecturer speaks and the audience listen without interrupting.

loan word   a word which is borrowed from another language. In English *café* is a borrowing from French, *bungalow* is a borrowing from Gujarati.

narrative   writing or talking that tells the story of something that happened. A narrative may be true, or it may be fiction.

narrator   the person who tells the narrative.

non-standard   using vocabulary or grammar in ways that are not correct for **Standard English**.

noun   nouns are words that refer to people, places, things and ideas: cake, thought, child, sand, butter, happiness, November.

novel   a story that takes up a whole book. A novel usually has a number of **characters** and the events in it take place in one or more **settings**.

object   in many sentences, the object comes after the verb. It refers to the person or thing that is affected by the action of the verb:
>   The dog bit *the postman*.

I've lost *the notebook with my maths home-work in it.*

phrase a group of words that makes sense, but not full sense on its own. A phrase does not contain a complete verb. Examples:
coffee ice- cream
playing football
the biggest aspidistra in the world
See **clause**.

plot the main events in a story and the way in which they are linked together.

point of view when something happens it can be reported in different ways according to who is telling the story. For example, if Mark and Imran have a row, Mark's version of what happened will be different from Imran's. If we are making up a story, we can choose to tell it from different points of view.

prefix an **affix** that comes at the beginning of a word:
In the words *preposition, prefix* and *preparation*, the prefix is *pre–*.

preposition prepositions come before nouns and adverbs. They are the 'little words' of English:
up the hill, *by* now, *for* example, *until* then

pronoun pronouns are used to stand instead of nouns. They help us to avoid too much repetition. Some of the commonest pronouns are:
I she he you we they it
me her him us them
my his our your their its
myself, himself, herself, ouselves, yourselves, themselves, itself
who whom whose that what which
this that these those

pronunciation the way in which a person speaks the words of a language.

proof-reading reading through something that someone has written and correcting all the mistakes of spelling, punctuation and grammar.

prose writing in ordinary sentences. Prose is different from **verse** or poetry.

pun a play on words. Often words have more than one meaning (or two different words are pronounced in the same way) and we can make jokes by playing with these meanings.

purpose how we write or speak is affected by the **audience** and the purpose we have: why we are writing or speaking to them and the effect we want to have on them.

question see **sentence types**.

question mark see page 175.

report a narrative that sets out in a straight-forward way what happened. (It also has a special meaning in the phrase 'school report'!)

rhyme when two words end with a similar sound pattern, they rhyme: for example sit/hit, house/grouse, examination/complication. Rhyme is often used in poetry.

rhythm the pattern of strong and weak beats in speech or writing. Rhythm is important in poetry, but it can be important in prose, too.

second (language) Some countries have several different first languages. So that people with different first languages can talk to each other, they have to learn a common second language. (For example, in India Hindi or English is many people's second language. In Britain people who do not have English as their first language, usually have it as their second language.)

semi-colon the punctuation mark ; . A semi-colon is used between two clauses in a sentence. It makes a stronger pause than a comma, but not as strong as a full stop. It is often used to separate two more or less equal parts of a sentence:
'You never knew where you were with him: some days he was charming to everybody; other days he was as miserable as sin.'

A semi-colon can also be used to separate items in a list, when the items are longer than a few words:
'The following are now forbidden in school: walking around with your hands in your pockets; talking to members of the opposite sex; listening to personal stereos; anything else the slightest bit enjoyable.'

sentence types   there are four main types of sentence:
> *Statement*: This is a statement.
> *Question*: What is the question?
> *Command*: Give me a command.
> *Exclamation*: What a wonderful idea that was!

short story   a story that is much shorter than a novel. Often short stories are short enough to be read at a sitting.

slang   casual language that is special to one group of people. (Examples of this are school slang, thieves slang, motorbike slang.) It is often not acceptable outside that group. If you use slang outside the proper group you may well be criticised or laughed at.

Standard English   the **dialect** of English that is used when speaking in formal situations, and normally in writing.

statement   see **sentence types**.

stem   the main part of a word, to which prefixes and suffixes can be added. In the words *superman* and *manly* the stem is *man*.

subject   the subject of a sentence tells us what it is about. In a statement sentence it comes at the beginning:

> *Miriam* is unhappy.
> *The big blue book on the table* is mine.

suffix   an affix that comes at the end of the word. In the words *manly* and *slowly*, the suffix is *–ly*.

syllable   words can be made up of one or more syllables. Roughly speaking you can work out how many syllables a word has by counting the number of 'beats' as you say it:
> 1 syllable – bat, school, bounced
> 2 syllables – batted, bouncing
> 3 syllables – unbuttoned, Barnstaple

typeface   the different form that letters can have in a printed book. These are examples of different typefaces:

typeface typeface typeface

verb   It is difficult to write a proper sentence without a complete verb. Most verbs will fit into one or more of these spaces:
> He ——————— it. (eg liked)
> She ——————. (eg is singing)
> It ————— good. (eg is)

verse   writing that uses **rhyme** and **rhythm**.

vocabulary   the words of a language, or a piece of speech or writing.

Acknowledgements

We are grateful for permission to reprint the following copyright material:

W.H. Auden: from *Collected Poems*, (1976), by permission of the publishers, Faber & Faber Ltd.
Patricia Beer: from *The Collected Poems*, (1990), by permission of the publishers, Carcanet Press.
Louise Bennett: *Selected Poems*, by permission of the publishers, Sangster's Book Stores Ltd.   **Ronald Blythe**: from *Akenfield: Portrait of an English Village*, (Allen Lane, The Penguin Press), © Ronald Blythe, 1969, by permission of Penguin Books Ltd., and Rogers, Coleridge & White Ltd.   **Joan Brookman**: first published in Ron Williams (Ed.): *Tales from the Bulldog*, (Bulldog Writers' Workshop, 1985) by permission of the author.
Charles Causley: from *Early in the Morning*, (Viking, 1986), by permission of David Higham Associates.
Arthur C. Clarke: from *Of Time and Stars*, (Gollancz, 1972), by permission of David Higham Associates.
Peter Dixon: from *Grow your Own Poems*, (1988), by permission of the publishers, Macmillan, London and Basingstoke.   **Mary Elting**: from *The Macmillan Book of the Human Body*, text © by Mary Elting, 1986, by permission of the publishers, Macmillan Publishing Company Inc.   **Richard Garrett**: from *Hoaxes and Swindles*, (1978), by permission of the publishers, Pan/Macmillan Children's Books.   **Goscinny-Uderzo**: from *Asterix and the Goths*, ©1990, Les Editions Albert René/Goscinny-Uderzo, by permission of Les Editions Albert René, Paris.   **Mick Gowar**: from *Third Time Lucky*, (Viking Kestrel), © Mick Gowar, 1988, by permission of Penguin Books Ltd.   **Gregory Harrison**: from *The Night of the Wild Horses*, (OUP, 1971), by permission of the author.   **Shirley Jackson**: from *Lottery and Other Stories*, (Robinson, 1988), by permission of A.M. Heath & Co. Ltd.   **Jan Mark**: from *Thunder and Lightenings*, (Kestrel Books, 1976), © Jan Mark, 1976 by permission of Penguin Books Ltd.   **Arthur Marshall**: from *I Say!*, (1976), by permission of the publishers, Hamish Hamilton Ltd.   **A.S. Mehdevi**: from *Persian Folk and Fairy Tales*, (1966),

Acknowledgements

(1976), by permission of the publishers, Hamish Hamilton Ltd. **A.S. Mehdevi**: from *Persian Folk and Fairy Tales*, (1966), by permission of the publishers, Chatto & Windus Ltd. **Spike Milligan:** from *Unspun socks from a Chicken's Laundry*, (Puffin, 1982), by permission of Spike Milligan Productions Ltd. **Trevor Millum**: from *Warning: Too Much Schooling Can Damage Your Health*, (E.J. Arnold, now Nelson, 1988), by permission of the author. **Judith Nicholls**: from *Midnight Forest*, (Faber), © Judith Nicholls, 1987, by permission of the author. **Grace Nichols**: from M. Styles & H. Cook (Eds.): *There's A Poet Behind You*, (A & C Black, 1988) by permission of Curtin Brown Ltd. **Michael Park**: first published in *Scarborough Top Trader*, Sept. 1988, by permission of the author. **Jack Prelutsky**: from *Nightmares: Poems to Trouble Your Sleep*, (1978), by permission of the publishers, A & C Black. **Peter Rowan**: from *Ask Doctor Pete*, (1986), by permission of the publishers, Jonathan Cape Ltd. **Christopher Rush**: from *A Twelvemonth and A Day*, (1985), by permission of the publishers, Aberdeen University Press. **William Saroyan**: from *Best Stories of William Saroyan*, by permission of Laurence Pollinger Ltd., on behalf of The William Saroyan Foundation. **Jonathan Swift**: from Paul Turner (Ed.): *Gulliver's Travels*, (1986), by permission of the publishers, Oxford University Press. **Robert Swindells**: from *The Moonpath and Other Stories*, (Arnold/Wheaton, now Nelson, 1979), by permission of Jennifer Luithlen on behalf of the author. **Simon Wiltshire**: first published in David Orme (Ed.): *Creative Writing*, (Stanley Thornes), by permission of the author. **Kit Wright**: from *Hot Dog and Other Poems*, (Kestrel Books, 1981), © Kit Wright, 1981, by permission of Penguin Books Ltd.

Also to: **Airtours plc** for advertisement for Caribbean holidays, **Associated Newspapers plc** for 'Fred Bassett' cartoon by **Graham** and heading, both from *The Daily Mail*. **British Broadcasting Corporation** for extracts from *Speak*, BBC Radio, and from *DEF II*, BBC Television. **The Consumers' Association** for extracts from *Which?*, August 1988. **Express Newspapers plc** for article from *The Daily Express*. **The Guardian** for article and weather forecast from *The Guardian*. **Mr Boyd Hill** for letter to The Independent. **Ideal Home** magazine for extract from *Beautiful Living* by **Linda Parker**. **Louis Newmark plc** for *Swatch* advertisement. **Newspaper publishing plc** for article from *The Independent Magazine*, Feb. 1989. **Oral-B Laboratories Ltd.**, for extract from information leaflet. **Rex Features** on behalf of News Group Newspapers Ltd., for headline from *The Sun*. **The Royal National Theatre** for theatre poster/Flash leaflet. **Tesco Stores Ltd.**, for extracts from two leaflets. **Times Newspapers Ltd.**, for heading from *The Times*, Jan. 1990. **Today** newspaper for sports logo and article by **George Campbell** from *Today*. **Unicef UK** for data from *The State of the World's Children*, 1987. And **Young Newspaper Pulbishing Ltd.**, for two articles from *The Indy*.

Although every effort has been made to trace and contact copyright holders before publication, we have not been successful in a few cases. If notified, the publishers will be pleased to rectify any omissions at the earliest opportunity.

The illustrations are by:
Tony Ansell p66, 68, 128, 129, 152; **Jane Campkin** p10; **Tony James Chance** p22, 51, 81, 83, 97, 98, 99, 100, 101, 102; **Frances Cony** p122 (top and middle); **James Dodds** p70; **Antonia Enthoven** p76; **Katey Farrell** p87, 88, 91, 122 (bottom), 123, 146; **Gerard Gibson** p115, 168, 169; **Robin Harris** p57, 58, 60, 61, 62, 63; **Nicola Heindl** p94; **Mike Hingley** p11; **Linda Jeffrey** p43, 44, 45, 46, 47; **Andrew Laws** p32, 34, 35, 84, 85; **John Levers** p12, 13, 16, 17, 137; **Diane Lumley** p25, 27, 28, 30, 154; **Rosemary Murphy** p92, 93, 127, 148, 149; **Mike Nicholson** p72, 73; **Oxford Illustrators** p140, 141, 142; **Abigail Pizer** p49, 50; **Julie Roberts** p86, 125, 144, 145; **Petra Rohr-Rouendaal** p114; **Rachel Ross** p6, 8, 9, 158, 159, 173; **Alan Rowe** p75, 136, 151; **Duncan Storr** p116, 117, 164, 166, 167; **Hannah Stuart** p55; **Stephen Wilkin** p37, 38, 40; **Barry Wilkinson** p109, 111, 113.

The handwriting is by **Elitta Fell** and **Luise Whiting**.

The publishers would like to thank the following for permission to reproduce photographs:

Richard George Allen p138; **Martyn Chillmaid** p21 (all), 79, 156, 157; **Oasis Films** p103, 104, 105, 106, 108; **Planet Earth Pictures, James Watt** p170; **John Seely** p133, 134, 135.

Oxford University Press, Walton Street, Oxford OX2 6DP

Oxford   New York   Toronto
Delhi   Bombay   Calcutta   Madras   Karachi
Petaling   Jaya   Singapore   Hong Kong   Tokyo
Nairobi   Dar es Salaam   Cape Town
Melbourne   Auckland

and associated companies in
Berlin   Ibadan

Oxford is a trademark of Oxford University Press

© John Seely, Frank Green and David Kitchen 1991
First published 1991
Reprinted 1991

ISBN 0 19 831162 1

Printed and bound in Great Britain by
Butler & Tanner Ltd, Frome and London